A. H Weston

The Rifle Club and Range

A. H Weston

The Rifle Club and Range

ISBN/EAN: 9783743308152

Manufactured in Europe, USA, Canada, Australia, Japa

Cover: Foto ©ninafisch / pixelio.de

Manufactured and distributed by brebook publishing software (www.brebook.com)

A. H Weston

The Rifle Club and Range

THE
RIFLE CLUB AND RANGE

By A. H. WESTON

WITH ILLUSTRATIONS

NEW YORK
HARPER & BROTHERS, PUBLISHERS
FRANKLIN SQUARE
1879

Entered according to Act of Congress, in the year 1879, by

HARPER & BROTHERS,

In the Office of the Librarian of Congress, at Washington.

PREFACE.

This work is intended to supply a long-needed and universally recognized want, and is placed before the public as the fruits of many years' experience, careful watching, and study, and of a belief in the practical obtainment of the requisite knowledge.

The author has endeavored to set forth in simple language, and as concisely as possible, plain facts and definite instructions for the organization of a Rifle Club or Association; the establishment of an open-air Rifle Range; the duties of the different officers, committees, etc.; and the complete method of successfully conducting matches and managing the affairs of the organization.

Information upon the subjects treated of in these pages has heretofore been almost wholly unobtainable. Rifle-shooting, upon a united plan, being still in its infancy in this country, as a consequence but a very limited number possess experience sufficient to instruct others. It is therefore confidently believed that the issue of this volume cannot fail to be productive of results beneficial to the cause.

From beginning to end the reader will notice this to be a continuous story, while the several "headings" and the "Table of Contents" will prove ready references to any particularly desired portion.

An advisory strain has been used only in matters of detail and general execution connected with management, the reader being left to his own judgment to decide upon the relative merits of the products of manufacturers, originators, or inventors.

It now only remains to be seen whether, by the publication and circulation of this book, the objective desires of its author will be gratified by the establishment of Rifle Clubs and Associations throughout the country—a realization of which will justify him in saying of the good to be accomplished, *Probatum est.*

A. H. W.

TABLE OF CONTENTS.

	Page
The Rifle Club	11
First Steps towards Organization	12
Committee on Constitution and By-laws	13
Incorporation	14
Blank Form of By-laws	16
Blank Certificate of Incorporation	24
The Rifle Range	26
Suitable Ground	28
Fence to Stop Bullets	30
Targets	33
" Iron (Creedmoor)	34
" " ("Running Deer")	45
" Stone	49
" Wood	49
" " ("Man")	50
" Sheet-iron	51
" Tin	51
" Paper	51
" Canvas	52
" " (Wimbledon)	53
" " (Brunel's)	57
" " (Sanford's)	60
" " (Double)	65
" " (Swinging)	65
" " (Jewell's)	68
" " (Revolving)	73
" " (the "Possible")	76
Targets Reduced	82
Marking and Spotting Disks	84
Paper Patches	85
Danger Signals	85
Trigger-testers	86

CONTENTS.

	Page
Wind-indicators	86
Scoring-boards	90
Programme of Prize Meeting	91
Form of Entry Blank	95
Estimated Expenses of Meeting	97
Estimated Receipts of Meeting	98
Prizes, Hints as to Obtaining	99
Secretary's Department	101
Competitor's Number	102
Team Number	103
Individual Entry Sheet	103
Team Entry Sheet	104
Executive Department	106
Target Assignment (Blank)	107
System of Assigning	108
Target Assignment (Filled Up)	110
Statistical Department	111
Financial Department	112
Pool and Bull's-eye Tickets	113
Range Officers	114
Committees	114
Prize Committee	115
Range Committee	115
Conduct of Simple Matches	116
General Instructions for Score-keepers	118
General Instructions for Markers	119
Regulations of the N. R. A.	120
Extract from By-laws of the N. R. A.	133
Forms of Score Tickets	135
Domestic Rifle Clubs and Associations	145
Foreign Rifle Clubs and Associations	153
Rifle Record—Scores in Europe and America	155
Ireland versus America, 1874 and 1875	155
Canada versus the United States, 1875	156
Centennial Trophy—First Match	156
Ireland versus America, 1876	158
Centennial Trophy—Second Match	159
Canada versus the United States, 1877	159
Centennial Trophy—Third Match	160
International Military Match	160
Inter-state Military Matches	162
Inter-state Long-range Matches	164

CONTENTS.

	Page
"Leech Cup" Matches	165
"Wimbledon Cup" Matches	166
"Champion's" Matches	166
Military Championship of the United States	167
"Judd" Matches	169
"Short-range" Matches	169
"Short-range Team" Matches	170
"Time" Matches	172
"Tramp" Match	172
"Soldier's" Match	173
Aggregate Prizes and Winners	174
"Elcho Challenge Shield" Matches	176
"The Queen's Prize" Matches	178

LIST OF ILLUSTRATIONS.

Diagrams of N. R. A. Targets.....................*Faces page*	11
Wimbledon Rifle Range (Plan)...............................	29
Bullet-proof Fence..	30
Creedmoor Rifle Range (Plan)................................	35
Embankment, Targets, and Butts at Creedmoor..............	37
Creedmoor Target and Butt (Section).......................	38
" " " (Front View)....................	40
" " " (Plan)...........................	42
Running Deer, Fence, etc.....................................	47
" " Target...........................	48
"Man" or "Time" Target....................................	50
Wimbledon Target and Butt (Section).......................	54
" " " (Front View)....................	55
Brunel's Target (Section)....................................	58
" " (Front View)	59
Sanford's Target (Section)...................................	62
" " (Front View)...........................	63
Swinging Targets (Front View)...............................	67
Jewell's Target (Front View).................................	69
" " (Attachment).....................	71
" " (Attachment).....................	72
Revolving Targets (Section)..................................	74
" " (Front View)...........................	75
The "Possible" Target (Section).............................	78
" " " (Front View).........................	80
Brinton Rifle Range (Plan)...................................	83
Marking-disks..	84
Dial Wind-indicator..	87
Walnut Hill Range (Plan).....................................	89
The American Centennial Trophy "Palma"..................	157
The "Hilton Trophy," International Military Prize..........	161
The "Soldier of Marathon," Inter-state Military Prize.......	163
The "Military Championship of the United States" Medal...	168

DIAGRAM OF TARGETS
IN USE UPON THE RANGE AT CREEDMOOR, L.I.
Adopted by the National Rifle Association of America, 1875.

FIRST-CLASS TARGET, 6 × 12 FEET.
All distances over 600 yards.

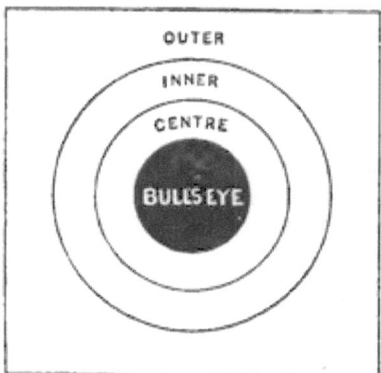

Bull's-eye, circular, 36 inches in diameter.
Centre,   "   54   "
Inner, square, 6 feet × 6 feet.
Outer, remainder of Target.

SECOND-CLASS TARGET, 6 × 6 FEET.
All distances over 300, to, and including, 600 yards.

THIRD-CLASS TARGET, 4 × 6 FEET.
All distances up to and including 300 yards.

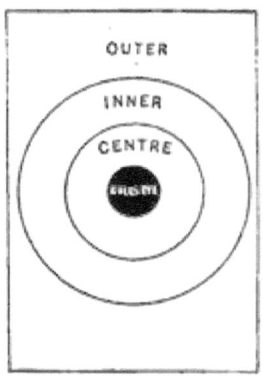

Bull's-eye, circular, 22 in. in diam.
Centre,   "   38 "   "
Inner,   "   54 "   "
Outer, remainder of target.

Bull's-eye, circular, 8 in. in diam.
Centre,   "   26 "   "
Inner,   "   46 "   "
Outer, remainder of target.

THE RIFLE CLUB AND RANGE.

THE RIFLE CLUB.

In every city, town, and village of these United States are to be found some who, either from a previous "taste" or from having read accounts of matches and tournaments elsewhere, have formed an undeveloped desire and ambition to handle a rifle before a target with other competitors. A few of these may have used a shot-gun, and by returning proudly home with a full bag of game have proved their skill in this direction. Others may be the happy possessors of rifles that they have rarely, if ever, fired; and others, again, may wish to have a rifle and to shoot with it, but are deterred from obtaining one by a knowledge of its uselessness without a range whereon to practise. To such, and in fact to all interested, a careful perusal of the following instructions and suggestions is recommended.

A rifle is a comparative "Crusoe's boat" without a place whereat to test it; and it is with a view to so clearly pointing out the manner of forming a Rifle Organization and establishing a Rifle Range that any few united and earnest persons can successfully do both that this work has been written.

Every new project or enterprise must have an originator, one to call attention to the proposed scheme and obtain supporters. Should this book fall into the hands of any one wishing to see the establishment of a Rifle Club or Association, *to him* I would say, *You yourself* take the initiatory steps, and give the project and enterprise a start, commencing in the following manner:

FIRST STEPS.

Call a meeting of as many eligible friends and acquaintances as will respond for a certain day or evening, at a certain hour, at your own house, or at Mr. A——'s house, or elsewhere.

State beforehand the object of the call, and try and obtain a friend, or friends, to co-operate with you. When all are assembled, rise and explain the objects of the meeting, and ask for support. Show them a copy of this little book, and move for the appointment of a chairman and secretary *pro tem*. You yourself nominate, as temporary chairman, some one whom you believe will favor and "push" the cause. Having organized your meeting, move the appointment of a committee of three (this number is enough) on Constitution and By-laws. If you are a "talker," talk to the meeting of rifle-shooting; tell them how, for many years, we Americans have boasted of our prowess with the rifle; of how it is the "national weapon;" of the historical feats of marksmanship performed by our forefathers during the Revolutionary wars; of our typical American hunters with their deadly rifles and unerring aim; of our citizen soldiers, upon whom the country relies for protection, etc.; and if you cannot move them with these arguments, if they are not in the humor to be "revived" by patriotic emotions, tell them of the pleasure and sport of rifle-shooting — how healthful, exhilarating, and recreative it is; how it conduces to a moral and prudent living; how it is elevating to a degree, requiring, as it does, an abstemious and careful living. Use these arguments, and combine with them any others of your own that may suggest themselves, and the chances are largely in favor of your wishes becoming gratified, and your Rifle Association being established even while the organization is but an embryo.

We will now suppose our committee of three on Constitution and By-laws to have been appointed, with instructions to report at the next meeting, to be held at Mr. B——'s house one week from to-night.

The first thing for this committee to do should be to appoint a time and place to meet again in, say, two days from the present time, each individual member of the committee, in the meantime, exerting himself to obtain a copy of the By-laws of one or more associations or clubs organized in your state, and, if possible, consulting with some lawyer (as laws of the various states, of course, differ) as to the proper steps to take to become a regularly and legally constituted body.

When the committee meet, let them compare notes, and draw up a set of By-laws consistent with the objects and aims, bearing in mind the necessity of acclimatizing, as it were, the duties and laws to harmonize with the peculiarities or requirements of your local surroundings. To enable an association or club so formed to hold property, it is necessary that the same be legally incorporated. This can be done in New York State by filing a certificate in the offices of the Secretary of State and County Clerk, stating the name and object of the Association or Club, the number of its directors, and the names of those who shall manage its affairs for the first year, which should be signed and acknowledged by all of the directors themselves. This certificate must also be approved, before filing, by a judge of the Supreme Court.

When an association or club is thus incorporated under the State Act provided for such cases, its members are not liable for any debts; and the liability of the directors is limited to debts payable within the year, or, in other words, to cash purchases. It is undesirable to have many meetings of the Association or Club; therefore a Board of Directors should have all power of management, and be elected annually.

The machinery for admission to membership should be as simple as possible. Complication of all kinds should be guarded against. In a word, try and think of everything necessary. Try to omit nothing in the By-laws that should be provided for. Amendments are always troublesome, and are generally the result of a too hasty adoption of the original.

The following blank form of By-laws has been compiled partly from the By-laws of the National Rifle Association of America, partly from the By-laws of other associations and clubs, and is partly original. It will, it is believed, cover nearly all points necessary, and prove a good and sound basis upon which to build a young and enterprising Rifle Organization. It has been prepared to adinit and cover military practice and support; but where an association is to be formed merely for amusement, the wording can be changed to conform to the object.

The word "Association" has been used in the following form, but "Club" can, of course, be substituted if desired.

BY-LAWS OF THE

NAME.

I. This Association shall be called the ——— ———.

OBJECT.

II. Its object shall be the encouragement of Rifle Practice among ——— ——— throughout ——— ———.

MANAGEMENT.

III. A Board of Directors, elected annually by the Association at its annual meeting, and consisting of ——— members, shall have general control of its affairs, take cognizance of all infractions of the By-laws, and fill vacancies in its own body until the time of the next annual meeting. The Board of Directors shall, from time to time, make such rules and regulations, not inconsistent with these By-laws, as it may consider necessary.

The Directors named in the Certificate of Incorporation shall be deemed to have been elected, and shall divide themselves by lot into three classes of ——— members each. The first class shall hold office until the ——— day of ——— 18—.* The second class

---

* Three years from date of first annual meeting of the Association.

BY-LAWS.

shall hold office until the —— day of ——, 18—;* and the third class shall hold office until the —— day of ——, 18—;† and thereafter, at each annual election, to be held on the —— —— in —— of each year, there shall be elected by and from the life members of this Association —— directors, to hold office three years, to supply the places of the class retiring, and for such additional number as may be necessary to fill vacancies to hold office during the remainder of the terms of the members whose places they fill.

QUORUM.

IV. A quorum of the Board of Directors shall consist of —— members.

OFFICERS AND COMMITTEES.

V. The officers of the Association shall consist of a President, Vice-President, Secretary, and Treasurer, who shall be elected annually, and of an Executive Officer, who shall be elected quarterly (or semi-annually) by the Board of Directors.

VI. The first three of the following standing committees shall be appointed by the President during the month of January in each year:

1st. Finance Committee,
2d. Range Committee, } Each to consist of three members.
3d. Prize Committee,

4th. The Executive Committee to consist of the officers of the Association and three directors elected annually by the Board.

DUTIES OF OFFICERS AND COMMITTEES.

VII. 1. The President, or, in his absence, the Vice-President, shall preside at all meetings of the Association, the Board of Di-

---

* Two years from date of first annual meeting of the Association.

† One year from date of first annual meeting of the Association.

rectors, and the Executive Committee; and shall perform such other duties as generally devolve upon presiding officers.

2. The Secretary of the Association shall notify each member of the Board of Directors of all its meetings, and each member of the Association of every meeting of the Association; issue all other authorized notices to members; make and keep a true record of all meetings of the Association, the Directors, and the Executive Committee; have custody of the books and papers and the corporate seal of the Association; conduct all correspondence; and make a monthly report to the Board of Directors, and an annual report to the Association.

3. The Treasurer shall collect and have charge of the funds of the Association, and pay such bills as have been audited by the Finance Committee and passed for payment by the Board of Directors. He shall keep accounts of all his transactions, and make a detailed report thereof, with vouchers annexed, at each regular meeting of the directors, and an annual report to the Association at its annual meeting. He shall give bonds in such sum as shall be fixed by the Directors.

4. The Finance Committee shall have general supervision of the finances of the Association. They shall from time to time examine the accounts of the Treasurer, and keep themselves informed of the financial condition of the Association. To this committee shall be referred the Treasurer's reports, and all questions and propositions relating to finances; and no obligations of the Association beyond those necessary for current wants shall be made until the Finance Committee have considered and reported upon the necessity and propriety of the plan proposed. They shall likewise audit all just claims against the Association before the same can be acted upon by the Board.

5. The Executive Committee may be convened upon call by the President or Vice-President, or upon the demand of any member.

All the powers and duties of the Board of Directors not herein delegated to the officers or to other committees shall be exercised and discharged during the recess of the Board by this committee.

Four members shall constitute a quorum. The minutes of their proceedings shall be recorded in a book kept for the purpose, and shall be reported to the Board of Directors for ratification after having been previously approved by the committee.

All the acts of the Executive Committee shall be binding upon the Association until disapproved by the Board of Directors at a regular meeting.

6. The Range Committee shall have charge of the grounds and all property of the Association upon the Range, and shall recommend to the Board of Directors such changes and improvements as in their judgment are necessary or desirable. They shall prescribe the duties and direct and regulate the services of all persons employed on the Range, and shall keep it supplied with all necessary articles. They shall certify to the correctness of all claims and bills against the Association for supplies used upon the Range, and sign all contracts; and no such bills, claims, or contracts shall be paid until so certified or signed. But this committee shall have no power to make contracts or purchases in the name of the Association for anything more than the usual supplies, unless the same be authorized and ordered by a formal vote of the Board of Directors.

They shall make quarterly returns of the property upon the Range, which returns shall show:

1st. The amount of property on hand last return.
2d. The amount received during the month.
3d. The amount to be accounted for.
4th. The amount expended.
5th. The amount sold.
6th. The amount lost or destroyed.
7th. The amount remaining on hand.
8th. The condition of such property.

Such returns shall be presented regularly to the Board of Directors for examination and filing. They shall make such temporary rules and regulations for the use of the ground and the targets as shall seem necessary to insure the most privileges to the greatest number. They shall see that contracts for work to be done and materials to be furnished, and agreements for rents and privileges at the Range, are faithfully executed, and generally do and perform everything needful to protect the interests of the Association and secure a successful management of the Range.

In case of any violation of the rules of the Range, the Range Committee shall have power to suspend the offender from the privileges thereof until the action of the Board of Directors. The committee shall report all such suspensions at the next meeting of the Board in writing, with the reasons for their action.

7. The Prize Committee shall select, procure, and assign the prizes obtained or offered by the Association.

MEETINGS.

VIII. The members of the Association shall hold an annual meeting on the —— of —— in each year, and such special meetings as may be called pursuant to these By-laws. If the annual meeting shall not take place at the time fixed, it shall be held as soon after as convenient, and the officers and directors whose terms of office have expired shall hold over until their successors are chosen.

It shall be the duty of the President, or, in his absence, of the Vice-President, to call a meeting of the Association on receiving a requisition signed by —— members or —— directors. In the notice calling any special meeting, the particular subjects to be considered shall be specified, and no other business shall be transacted at such meeting but that specified in the notice.

—— members present at a general or special meeting shall constitute a quorum for the transaction of business.

At no meeting of the Association shall any subject be introduced or discussed which does not relate directly to its affairs.

The regular meetings of the Board of Directors shall be held on the —— —— of each month. Special meetings may be called at any time by the President, or, in his absence, by the Vice-President, and shall be called by either of them upon the request of —— members.

Upon the appearance of a quorum at the time appointed for any regular meeting of the Association or Board, the President, or, in his absence, the Vice-President—or if neither be present, a member selected to preside—shall call the meeting to order and proceed in the following

ORDER OF BUSINESS.

1. Calling the roll.
2. Reading minutes of previous meetings not passed upon.
3. Reports from the Secretary, Treasurer, Finance, Range, and Prize committees and select committees.
4. Unfinished business.
5. New business.

Neglect on the part of any Director to attend six successive meetings of the Board shall be deemed a tender of his resignation of office. But the Board may excuse any member for such neglect; and before his resignation is accepted under this By-law, the member in default must be specially notified of the same.

INSPECTION OF RECORDS AND ACCOUNTS.

IX. Any Director, or any member of the Association, may at any time examine the records of the Secretary, and inspect the accounts of the Treasurer.

MEMBERSHIP.

X. Any person giving his name, age, address, and the name of the military organization (if any) with which he is connected, shall, upon paying the sum of —— dollars, become a member of the Association for that year, subject to the right of the Board of Directors to reject his name and return his dues, in case the Board shall deem it required by the interests of the Association.

Any person may become a member for life upon payment, in one sum, of —— dollars, and upon being duly elected by the Board of Directors.

Regiments, companies, troops, and batteries of the regular Army, Navy, uniformed militia, or National Guard of any state, shall be entitled to constitute all their regular members in good standing members of this Association, on the payment of one half the annual dues for the current year for each member present at the last annual inspection.

RIGHTS AND DUTIES OF MEMBERS.

XI. No member shall be allowed to transfer his rights of membership.

All members shall be entitled to equal rights and privileges upon the Range.

Life members only shall be entitled to vote at any meeting of the Association.

Any member who shall have violated any of the rules of the Range, or whose conduct shall be pronounced by vote of the Board of Directors to have endangered, or be likely to endanger, the welfare, interest, or character of the Association, shall forfeit his membership. Such vote shall not be taken without giving two weeks' notice to the offender of the charges made against him, and affording him an opportunity of being heard in his defence. No person so removed shall be eligible for membership unless his disability be removed by vote of the Board.

No member shall take any property whatsoever belonging to the Association from its rooms or grounds, except on the authority of a resolution of the Board of Directors or Executive Committee.

No Director shall receive any profit, salary, or emolument from the funds of the Association, on any pretence, or in any manner whatsoever.

No member shall give any gratuity to any servant of the Association.

All rights and interests of a member in the property and privileges of the Association shall cease with the termination of his membership.

THE RIFLE RANGE.

XII. The Rifle Range shall be under the immediate direction of the Range Committee.

Members in arrears for dues or fines shall not be entitled to the use of the Range.

No betting shall be allowed on the grounds of the Association.

AMENDMENT OF THE BY-LAWS.

XIII. To amend these By-laws, the proposed amendment shall be subscribed to by at least —— members, and by them presented to the President, who shall cause such amendment, with the signatures thereto, to be brought before the Board of Directors at its next meeting. In case the Directors, by a majority vote, recommend its passage, the Secretary shall issue notices enclosing a copy of the amendment to all life members of the Association, and a vote in favor of the proposed amendment, of two thirds of all the life members present at the next annual meeting on the —— of ——, or at a special meeting to be called for the purpose, shall be requisite for its passage.

The following is the form of Certificate of Incorporation used in New York State:

BLANK CERTIFICATE OF INCORPORATION.

State of New York, } ss.
City and County of ———.

Know all men by these presents that we, the undersigned, ——— ——— ——— ——— ——— ——— ——— ———, being citizens of the United States and the State of New York, do hereby, pursuant to, and in conformity with, an act of the Legislature of the State of New York entitled "An act for the formation of societies or clubs for certain social and recreative purposes," passed on the eleventh day of April, eighteen hundred and sixty-five, and the various acts of said Legislature amendatory thereof, associate ourselves together, and form a body politic and corporate, and do hereby certify—

I. NAME OR TITLE.

That the corporate name by which said Society shall be known in law shall be ——— ———.

II. OBJECT.

The object for which said Association is formed is the encouragement of Rifle Practice among ——— ——— throughout ——— ———.

III. NUMBER OF DIRECTORS.

That the number of Directors of said Association who shall manage the same shall be ———.

IV. NAMES OF DIRECTORS.

That the names of the Directors of said Association who shall manage the same for the first year of its existence, are as follows: ——— ——— ——— ——— ——— ——— ——— ——— ———

In witness whereof, we have hereunto affixed our names, at the City of ———, this ——— day of ———, eighteen hundred and ——— ———.

——— ——— ——— ———
——— ——— ——— ———

INCORPORATION.

STATE OF NEW YORK, } ss.
CITY AND COUNTY OF ———.}

At various times between the —— day of —— and the —— day of ——, A.D. eighteen hundred and —— ——, before me personally appeared —— —— —— —— —— —— —— ——, known to me to be the persons described in, and who executed, the foregoing certificate, and duly signed the said certificate before me, and severally acknowledged that they executed the same for the purpose therein mentioned.

—— —— ——,

(*Seal.*)   Notary Public, County of ——.

I do hereby consent and approve of the incorporation of the —— —— under the within certificate.
Dated —— ——.

—— —— ——,

             Justice.

STATE OF NEW YORK, } ss.
CITY AND COUNTY OF ———.}

I, —— ——, Clerk of the said City and County, and Clerk of the Supreme Court of said State for said County, do certify:

That I compared the annexed with the original Certificate of Incorporation of the —— —— on file in my office, and that the same is a correct transcript therefrom, and of the whole of such original.

In witness whereof I have hereunto subscribed my name, and affixed my official seal, this —— day of —— 18—.

—— —— ——,

(*Seal.*)   Clerk.

State of New York, } ss.
Office of Secretary of State. }

I have compared the preceding with the original Certificate of Incorporation of the —— ——, with acknowledgment thereto annexed, filed in this office on the —— day of ——, 18—, and hereby certify the same to be a correct transcript therefrom, and of the whole of said original.

(Seal.)

Witness my hand and the seal of office of the Secretary of State, at the City of Albany, this —— day of ——, one thousand eight hundred and ——.

—— —— ——,
Secretary of State.

The Committee on Constitution and By-laws having made their draft form, present it at the next meeting (which was at Mr. B——'s house, we recollect); and, after having been read over, and the views of those present obtained, the motion is made, seconded, and carried that the By-laws, as submitted and amended (if any amendments), be adopted as a whole. The next thing to be done is to carry out the laws that have been adopted, do what is necessary to secure the incorporation, and then this first great stride towards the establishment of a Rifle Association is complete.

THE RIFLE RANGE.

As soon as the Association or Club is incorporated and has adopted its By-laws, the first question to arise will be the securing of a suitable Range, and to provide funds for its equipment. The main expense besides the land will be for targets. As in the infancy of the Association the ground may not be used all the time, it might be better and easier to lease it than to purchase it (unless, indeed, a good chance offered, and finances would permit of the latter). During the winter season, in addition to collecting funds, the influence of the Association or Club should be exerted to induce the National Guard, or troops in the State or vicinity, to practise aiming, drill, and gallery-shooting, as being most important steps towards the attainment of proficiency in marksmanship. If this is entered upon systematically, by the time weather will permit of practice in the open air a reasonable degree of proficiency will have been obtained, an interest taken in the subject, and the Association and its objects placed before the public more satisfactorily and creditably than could have been done by any other means. The tuition thus received will not only make the shooting better than it could possibly otherwise have been, and so give encouragement, but the arrangements for and conduct of matches can be more easily carried out upon the Range than if the competitors had had no previous experience.

The matter of obtaining aid from your State cannot be elaborated here, but will be best appreciated by those having the interests of rifle-shooting and of their own Association at heart.

There are at the time of writing thirty-two rifle ranges in the State of New York receiving official recognition and aid from the State authorities.

The first point—and a most essential one—to be considered in locating an open-air Range should be to secure ground that runs north and south, or nearly so—that is, targets at the north and shooters at the south. The reason for this may be briefly explained by the fact that in any other direction the *light* will be unsuited, and *shadows* probably fall across the targets.

Another great aim in selecting ground should be, if possible, a *natural embankment* or hill back of the targets to stop the bullets.

At Creedmoor much money was spent in raising an artificial embankment of earth, twenty-five feet above the level, with a bullet-proof fence ten feet high placed on top of that.

Artificial embankments, or contrivances to stop the bullets, can be built of earth, masonry, or a bullet-proof fence. The two first are understood; of the latter it may be said that a bullet-proof

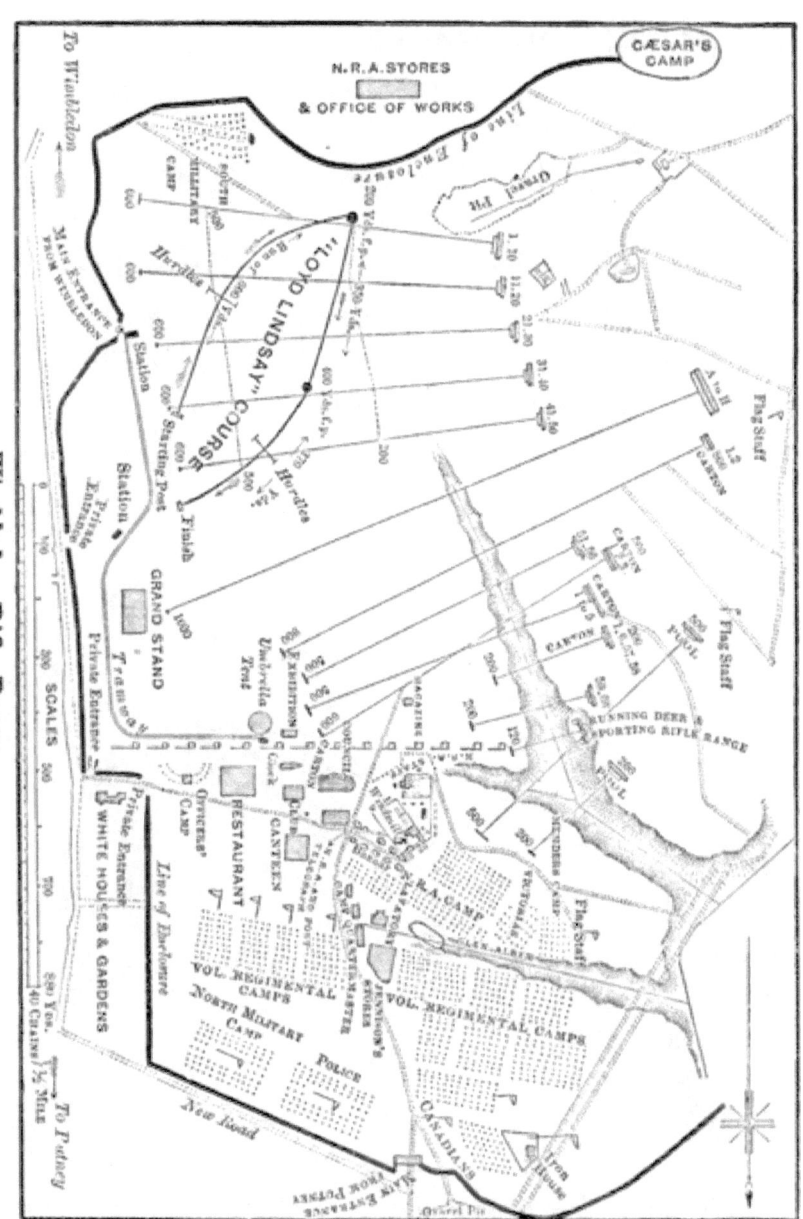

fence is generally made by filling in between plank loose stones or sand, sufficiently compact and wide to stop the bullets.

The fence should be made of good two-inch plank laid horizontally, and securely nailed to upright beams placed firmly in the ground outside of the planking, and half as many feet apart as the planks are long, the vacuum between the two plank walls being filled in with stone or sand.

Bullet-proof Fence, with end open, showing stone filling.

The supporting beams may in time be shot away, but, being outside, can be readily repaired. They should be bound together at the top by iron. The plank should be laid with the "joints broken," or (for the benefit of those who do not understand this term) fastened as bricks are laid. The height required, of course, depends upon circumstances. The width for a fence of moderate height should be about two feet at the top and three feet at the bottom, and may be braced or guyed with wood or wire rope front or back or both.

Level, dry ground is what is best suited for the purposes of a Rifle Range, though shooting can be, and is, done on many Ranges where dry and level ground is not obtainable, over a valley, marsh, or stream. It sometimes becomes necessary to construct *raised firing-points* to be on a level with the targets. These can be made either by grading, or (what is much cheaper) by erecting a wooden platform or scaffold of the required elevation. A mound, one or two feet high, should be built in front of the targets to catch ricochets. Though generally made of earth, asphaltum or a similar substance will answer the purpose better, for the reason that, by using such a compound, the bullet, when it strikes, will either bury itself within the mass, or, if it glance off, will do so without scattering dirt in every direction, which obscures the glass at an iron target, or, in wet weather especially, besmears the target itself. Easy and quick access between the targets and firing-points should also be considered.

Shade trees along the sides, or at southern end of the Range, are desirable. An abundant supply of good water must be on the ground; and if not obtainable by any other means, a well must be bored.

Good facilities to reach the Range from your city or town by rail or water, and within a reasonable time, should also be taken into consideration as of the most vital importance.

For present purposes the Range should not, if possible, be less than 550, nor need it be over 1050, yards in length. This will allow of extreme shooting at 500 in the first and 1000 yards in the second place, and all intermediate distances. The military rarely shoot at distances over 500 yards; while, for one rifleman who can and does shoot at extreme distances of 800 yards and over, there are one hundred who shoot only at the shorter ranges. By this it is not intended to imply that long-range shooting should be discouraged, but simply that for a youthful and inexperienced association the undisputed and time-honored fact should be borne in mind that to "reach the top of the ladder, we must commence to climb at the bottom." The system and probable number of targets to be adopted and erected must also be thought of, as upon these depends very largely the necessary width of the Range.

Without going into details of the purchase or lease and subsequent laying-out of ground (in which matters the services of a lawyer and practical surveyor or civil engineer should be respectively obtained), we will go on and see some of the different targets in use at the present time. Targets have been made of iron, canvas, wood, sheet-iron, stone, paper, etc., and each has its supporters. At Creedmoor the iron targets have always been used, and have given the most general satisfaction, despite sundry experiments with canvas and stone. Those first erected were imported from England, but our American manufacturers have now succeeded in fully equalling those of foreign make. It has always been desirable to keep *all* firing-points *on the same line*, instead of moving competitors back to increase the distance. This at Creedmoor, with the iron targets as they at present stand, is impracticable. Consequently, with the targets all on one line, the shooters are compelled to move forward or backward to lessen or increase the distance between targets and firing-points. While not offering any positive advice, or going very elaborately into details (which, if desired, can probably be obtained by corresponding with the inventors or manufacturers), the following diagrams are inserted showing the plain mechanical working, and giving general ideas of construction of the various plans and designs, commencing with the

TARGETS AT CREEDMOOR.

These are made of chilled-faced cast-iron slabs, each 2 feet by 6 feet, and $1\frac{1}{4}$ inches thick, ribbed on the back to keep them from warping. Standing two slabs together, we have the size of a third-class target, which only requires painting to make it ready for use. Three slabs form a second-class and six slabs a first-class target. Each slab weighs about 650 lbs., and usually requires four men to handle it. They are painted white on the face with a whitewash brush, a mixture of lime, water, and salt being used for the purpose. A pair of wooden compasses are then made use of to mark the circular bull's-eye, "centre," and "inner" divisions, after which the lines so traced are painted over with a mixture of lampblack and water or stale beer, a small brush being used for this purpose. The

Plan of Creedmoor Rifle Range,

The property of the National Rifle Association of America, situate at Creedmoor, Long Island, State of New York.

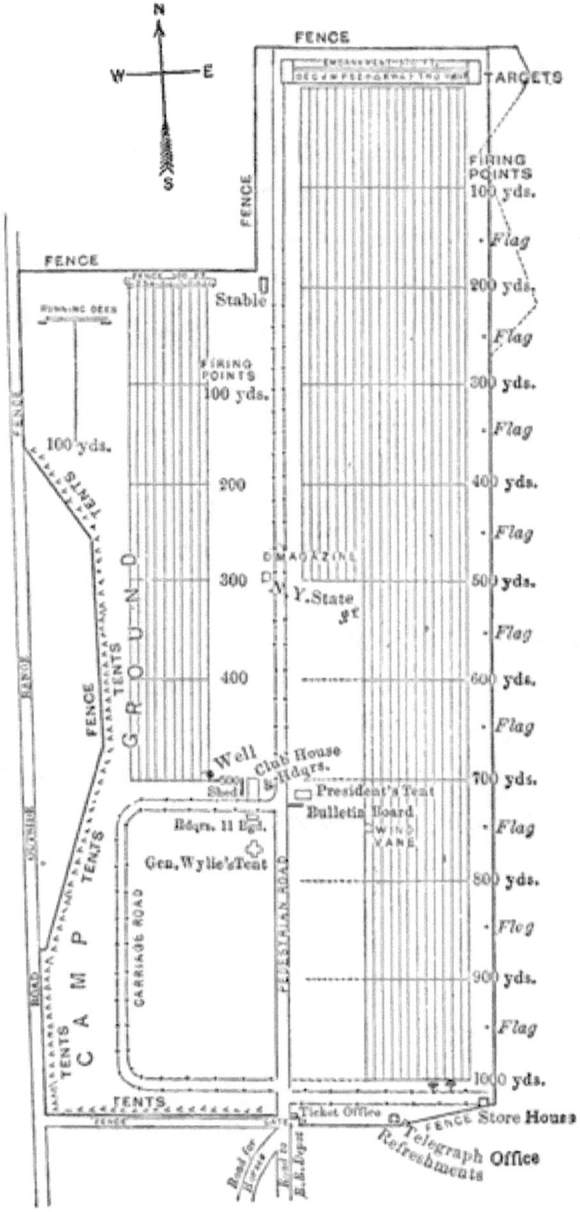

NOTE.—The dots on side of roads show trees.

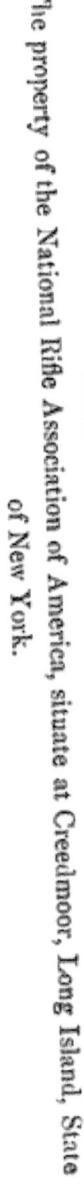

circle lines of the centre and inner divisions are striped about one quarter of an inch in width, and, if painted with coach-black and turpentine, will not so readily be erased in wet weather. The same white and black mixtures are used with the marking-disks for painting out shots on the targets.

At the determined point, so many hundred yards from the proposed firing-point, a pit or trench is dug, extending continuously along the line of as many targets as are to be erected; and when completed, the marker stands in this pit watching through a glass window the target above and in front of him.

Plate 1, on opposite page, gives a general idea, and shows a perspective view of the targets and butts (as much as can be seen of them from the outside), and plates 2, 3, and 4, on following pages, show scaled sections and plans.

PLATE 1.

General View of Embankment Fence, Targets, and Butts at Creedmoor, showing Entrance to Butts at one End.

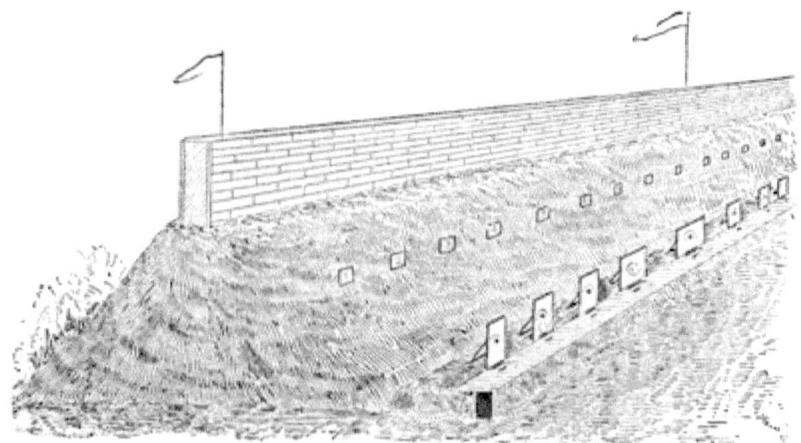

PLATE 2.

Section of Butt as built at Creedmoor, with Trap Closed.

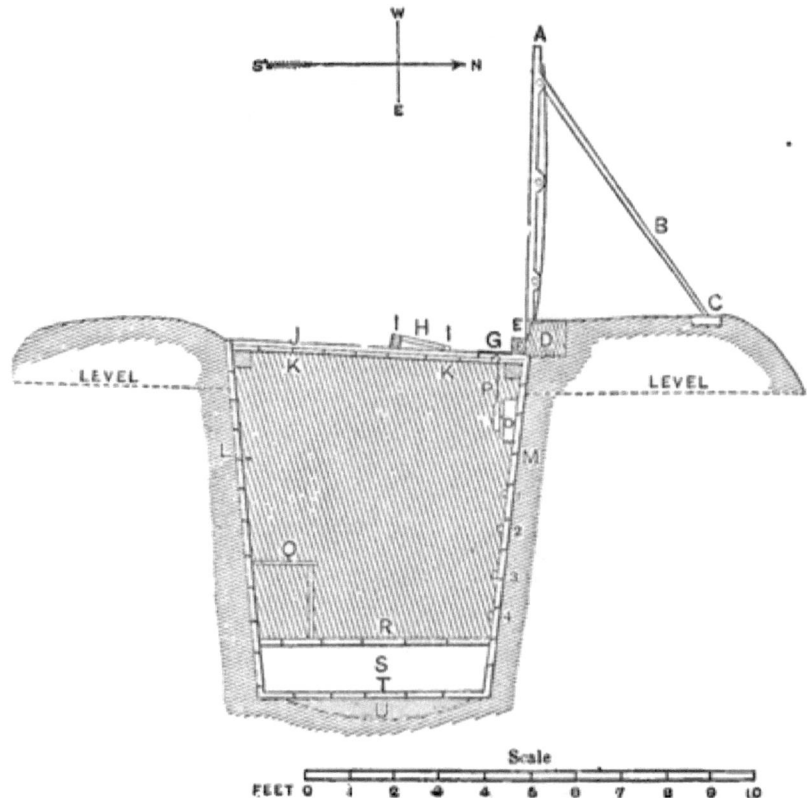

Explanation of Plate 2.

A, the iron target, 6 feet high.

B, iron brace of target (two braces to each *slab*) resting on

C, a piece of timber.

D, wooden sleeper upon which target rests, 8 by 8 inches thick and 6 feet long, for second- and third-class targets, and 12 feet long for first-class targets.

E, angle iron, $\frac{1}{4}$ inch thick, to protect woodwork from bullets.

F, wood, 5 inches high, $2\frac{1}{2}$ inches thick, on which trap is hinged.

G, the iron trap, down.

H, the glass window; plate-glass, 12 by 24 inches, $\frac{3}{4}$ inch thick.

I I, framework (wood) of window.

J, roof of butt, $1\frac{1}{4}$-inch plank, laid north and south.

K K, roof of butt, 2-inch plank, laid east and west.

L, south side or wall of butt, 2-inch plank, laid east and west.

M, north side or wall of butt, 2-inch plank, laid east and west.

O, wood on which trap-lever works.

P, trap—rod iron.

Q, marker's seat.

R, raised platform under each target; plank laid east and west.

S, plank or beam supporting platform.

T, floor of butt; plank laid east and west.

U, drain dug out; 1, 2, 3, and 4, racks for marking-disks.

PLATE 3.

Front View of Target and Butt as used at Creedmoor.

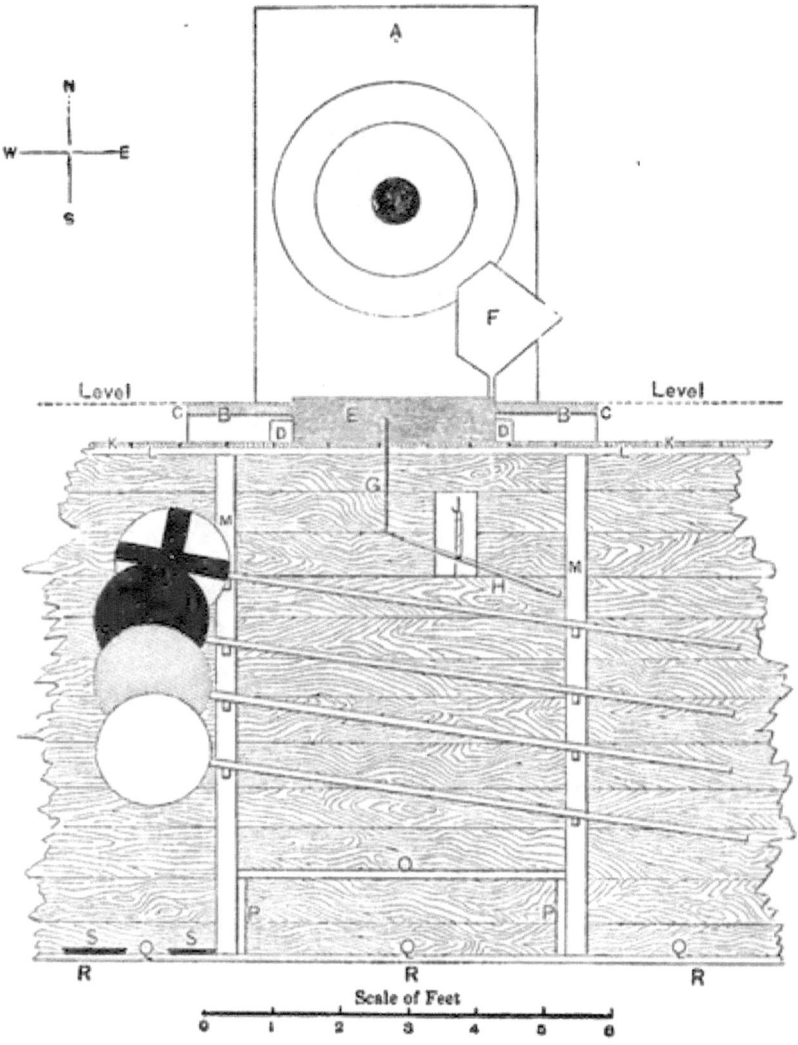

Explanation of Plate 3.

A, the iron target.
B B, wooden sleeper upon which target rests.
C C, angle iron protecting wooden sleeper.
D D, wood on which trap hinges.
E, the iron trap raised and open.
F, the sheet-iron trap-disk raised, painted red.
G, iron trap-rod.
H, handle of trap-lever.
I, pivot on which trap-lever works.
J, wood supporting trap-lever and pivot.
K, roof of butt; planks laid north and south.
L, inside roof of butt; planks laid east and west.
M M, stanchions supporting roof strengthening the walls of butt, and on which are placed racks for the marking-disks.
O, raised platform under each target.
P, planks or beams supporting platform.
Q, floor of butt.
R, drain dug out under butt.
S, white and black paint-pans for marking disks.

PLATE 4.

Plan of Butt with Iron Target as Used at Creedmoor.

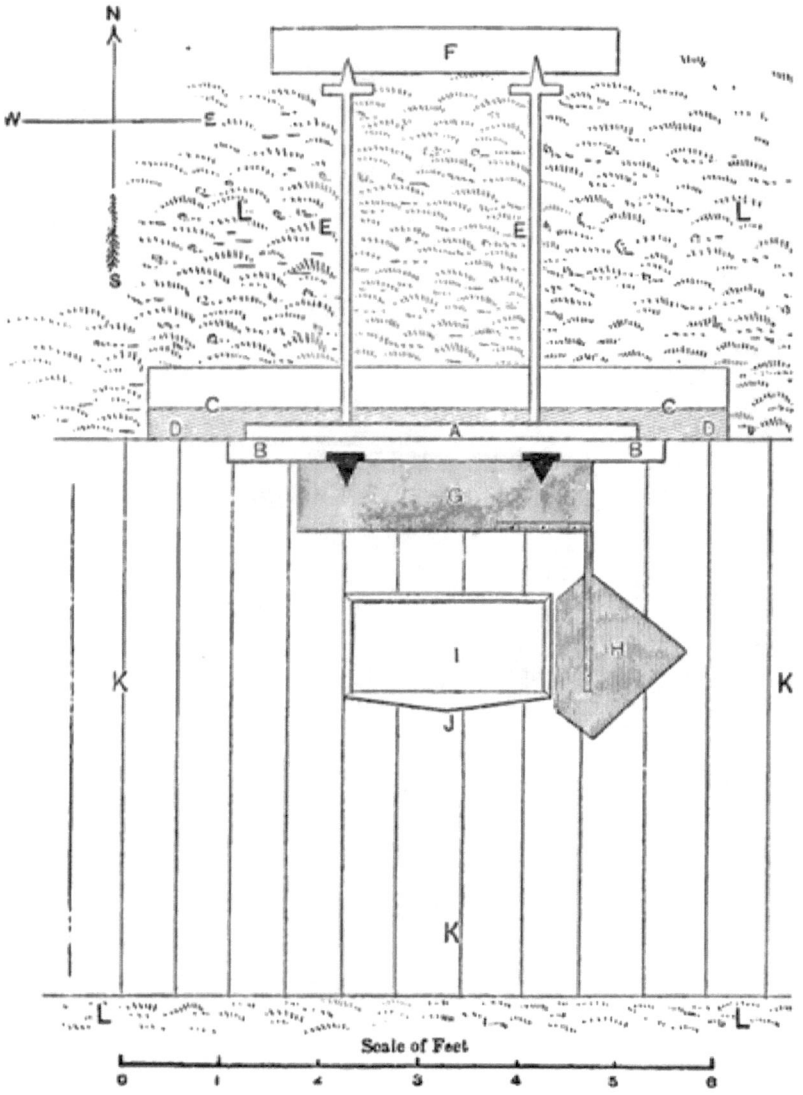

Explanation of Plate 4.

A, the iron target.
B B, woodwork upon which the trap hinges.
C C, wooden sleeper supporting target.
D D, angle iron protecting wooden sleeper.
E E, iron braces, holding target.
F, timber upon which braces rest.
G, iron trap, closed.
H, sheet-iron trap-disk, down.
I, plate-glass window.
J, framework of window.
K, roof of butt.
L, ground level with roof.

The really indispensable equipments upon a range with the above system of targets may be enumerated as follows: For each target four marking-disks, one danger-signal or flag, two paint-pans; and in the butts a supply of black and white paint, water in pails, compasses, brushes, some rags or paper to clean off the glass window if it should become obscured, etc.

At the firing-points as many danger-flags as there are targets; camp-stools or chairs; bugle, whistle, or other signal to call attention of markers; water-pails and tin-dippers; 3-lb. and 6-lb. trigger-testers; and at least one tent or shelter for statistical, financial, and other work, bulletin-board, etc. Additions to the above can, of course, be made in time.

The different firing-points (if not on one line) may be best designated by driving into the ground short stakes, about a foot high, painted white, each one in a direct line opposite its target, and bearing a painted number to correspond with the number thereof. A row of these stakes at, say, 200, 300, 400, and 500 yards will show the firing-points at those distances very plainly; and if a competitor is assigned to shoot at a certain target at a certain distance, he can, thus guided, readily proceed to the point designated.

A telephone, if obtainable, will be found very useful for purposes of communication between the firing-points and targets.

In addition to the regular targets at Creedmoor, there is likewise upon that range a "Running-Deer" Target, which affords much amusement for those sportively inclined, though, besides being a source of amusement, shooting at a moving object is really of considerable importance in developing in marksmen quickness of aim and promptness of action. Magazine guns are specially adapted for this class of shooting, as high as six or seven shots having been fired while the "deer" is running within the boundary lines a distance of seventy-five feet. In matches at the Running Deer, "any rifle—but sights to be over the centre of the barrel"—is generally allowed, the target being one hundred yards distant. The figure of a "Running Man," or, in fact, any other design that may be wished, can of course be substituted for the "deer." The figure is made of two thicknesses of iron (of similar manufacture to the target slabs), riveted together and working on a central pivot, which is held or carried by an iron-bound framework truck, running upon four wheels — grooved like the wheels of a common car—and running in turn upon steel or iron rails, partly by force of gravitation and partly by an impetus given it at the start on the down grade. After running down and up the inclined plane, the marker at the opposite side paints out with a brush the shot-mark (if a hit); signals with his disk, on the "dummy" painted on the wall, its location and value; turns the deer round on its pivot, so that it will not run backwards, and is ready, upon hearing the signal, to give it the required push sending it to the other side. Marking at this target is done with two small disks painted on each side respectively *white*, *red*, *black*, and *black cross on white background*. The first denotes a bull's-eye, counting 4; the second, a centre, counting 3; the third, an outer, counting 2; and the fourth, a "haunch," or hit on some part of the figure outside the outer line, counting 0, but being punishable by a fine of ten cents, which fine, together with fines of a similar amount for firing when the deer is out of bounds, or for not firing at all while it runs, are collected before another shot is fired.

It is here suggested that the signal for a "haunch shot" be a *red* cross on a white background, instead of a *black* cross, as used at Creedmoor. The latter, being the same signal as the "inner" at other targets, often causes confusion in scoring.

The divisions on the target are scaled as follows:

Bull's-eye, circular, 8 inches in diameter.
Centre,   "   22   "   "   "
Outer, any part of deer outside centre line within line dividing the haunch.

The following diagrams illustrate the construction and dimensions of the target, fence, and wings:

PLATE 5.

Running-Deer Target.

(FRONT VIEW.)

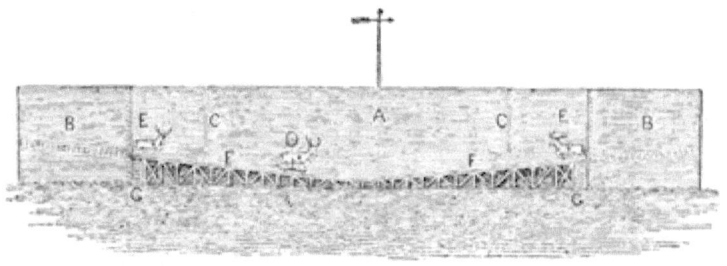

A, bullet-proof fence (plank filled in with stone), 112 feet long, 22 feet high, 2 feet wide at top, and 3 feet wide at bottom.

B B, wings, 25 feet long, 22 feet high, same width as main fence, and made in same manner. Placed about 3 feet in advance, and covering ends of main fence about one foot.

C C, painted "boundary lines," 75 feet apart, while running between which the deer may be shot at.

D, the "deer" running on the track.

E E, dummies of the deer painted on main wall, on which marker places the disk, showing where the deer itself has been struck.

F, the track, continuing at dotted lines behind the wings. A wooden platform for the marker's use is also built behind each wing, and level with the track at these points.

G G, steps leading to platforms at back of wings.

PLATE 6.

Running-Deer Target.

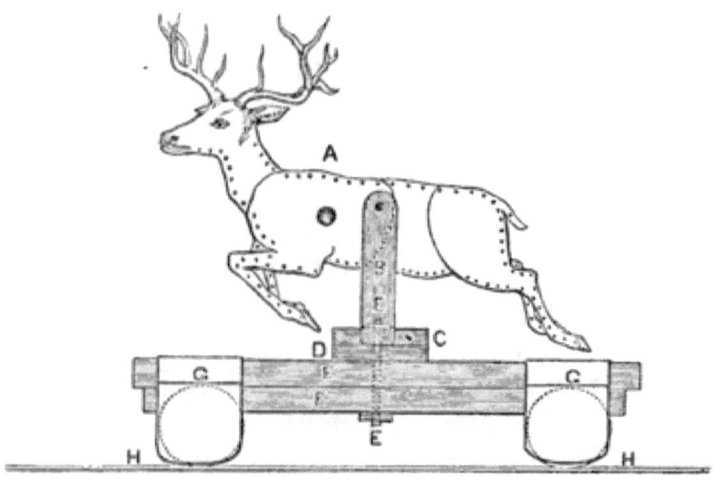

A, the "deer."

B, iron post (one each side) upon which deer hangs on pivot, strongly fastened to

C, a round plate of iron working upon

D, a similar round plate, fastened to the truck by an iron pin piercing both plates, and fastened at top and bottom by

E E, the nuts.

F F, wooden body of the truck or carriage covered with iron.

G G, thick iron covering protecting wheels.

H, the rails.

NOTE.—A thick iron protection must also be made covering the central pin or pivot and circular plates. By using a small straight spring or catch to fit in a cut in upper circular plate, it will prevent the deer from *turning round*, except when desired.

We now pass on to the

STONE TARGETS.

But one of these has ever been used at Creedmoor, and, though it retains its clearness and whiteness even in wet weather better than the iron target, the bullets chip away the stone, and it has been found too unwieldy for general purposes, requiring the united strength of eight or ten men to move it. Another objection to the stone target lies in the fact that it is unalterable, *i. e.*, cannot be changed to any class target at will, being one solid block of sandstone.

WOODEN TARGETS.

Of these targets but little need be said. They are easily made, easily covered with paper, easily moved, and—easily shot to pieces. Therefore, though they will answer well enough for a limited few to shoot at occasionally, they should not be considered permanently in connection with an established Range. As an interesting accessory, however, wooden targets may be used to advantage in "time" matches or "volley-firing."

The figure of a man, for instance, may be drawn or painted on paper and tacked or pasted on the wood, and worked with hinges like a door, conditions requiring competitors to fire as many shots

"Man" or "Time" Target.

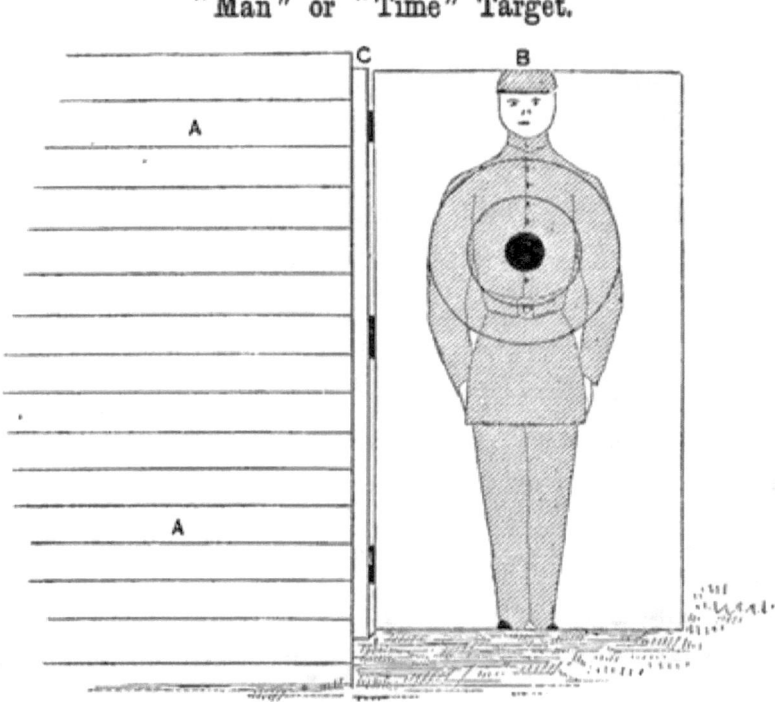

A, the protection behind which the marker stands, and, with a string or rod fastened to the bottom of

B, the target (with figure on it), closes or pushes it open like a door working upon hinges fastened to

C, an upright post driven in the ground.

as they please while the figure remains in view —for, say, thirty seconds.

A bullet-proof fence should be placed at a distance from the target towards the firing-point equal to its width; *i. e.*, if the target is 3 feet wide, the fence should be placed 3 feet from the target and on a line with the right or left edge of the target, which swings upon iron hinges, as before said, like a door.

The bullet, of course, passes through the paper and wood; and the marker, after pasting a piece of paper over the hole, shows with his disk (by placing it over the shot-mark) the value of the shot—"bull's-eye," "centre," and "inner" being divided by circular lines, and "outer" being allowed for a shot on any other portion of the body.

SHEET-IRON OR TIN TARGETS,

that is to say, wooden or other frames, covered with sheet-iron, tin, or other metal, have been made and used, but have been found too expensive, and without sufficient durability to have received much, if any, favor.

PAPER TARGETS.

These, likewise, for steady open-air rifle-shooting are comparatively worthless, being likely to tear, blow away, or turn into rags in wet weather. For indoor shooting, however, they are unsurpassed when pasted or tacked on wood.

We have now come to the

CANVAS TARGET,

the greatest rival of the iron. Many upholders has the canvas target, who claim for it cheapness, durability, safety, and easiness of handling. By "canvas" is meant any textile fabric applicable to the purpose.

But two disks are needed for a canvas target, as there are no brushes in the back, and they can be painted both sides—thus: white on one side, and red on the other; black cross on one side, and black on the other, representing respectively the bull's-eye, centre, inner, and outer.

Black and white patches of paper, about three inches square or round, for pasting over the bullet-hole made in the black or white portion, are used with all canvas targets.

The canvas is stretched upon a framework, generally of iron, triangular in shape, one angle facing the shooter, so that if the bullet strikes the iron, it will be *cut in two*, and pass on without "splash."

Wood, hoop-iron, and cane have also been tried for frames, the former of which is still used considerably. The canvas is usually fastened to an iron frame by strings, passing through holes bored in the iron, and tied. On a wooden frame it may either be tied or tacked. To avoid errors in marking, it is well to paste paper over the canvas, a bullet passing through which makes *more noise* than in passing through canvas alone, and can hardly escape the marker's notice.

The first to be described is the

WIMBLEDON TARGET,

as used upon the Range of the National Rifle Association of Great Britain at Wimbledon. The target works in a somewhat similar manner to the sashes of a window, the upper sash representing the target, and the lower sash a "dummy," or second target, covered with wire, and only used for signalling purposes.

It, however, differs from the principle of a window, inasmuch as when the target is pulled down the "dummy" goes up simultaneously.

The following plates, copied from the Annual Report of the National Rifle Association of 1875, are fac-similes thereof, except that the modern divisions on the target have been substituted for those of that year.

PLATE 7.
The Wimbledon Target.

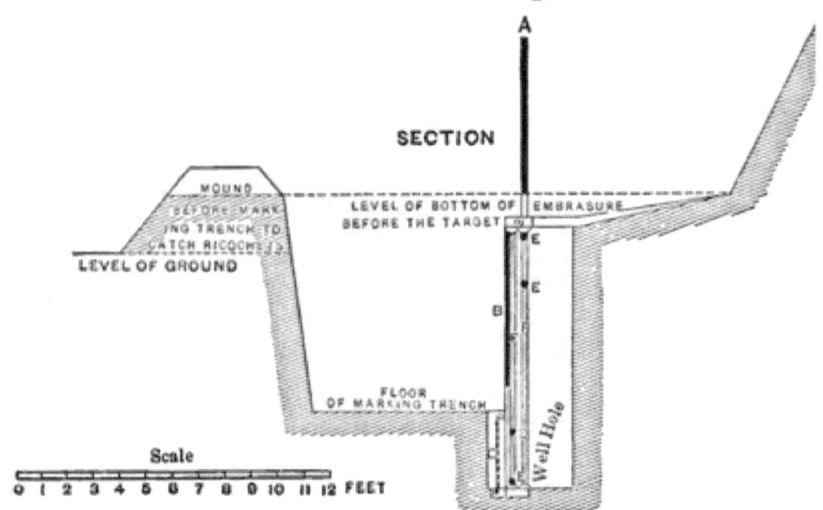

Explanation of Plates 7 and 8.

A, the target. Frame of iron (one inch thick by two inches deep, the front edge sharpened), covered with papered canvas.

B, the dummy, or signalling target. Frame of wood, or of iron same as above, covered with board or canvas. Over the face of the dummy is stretched a wire net, and to the top a danger-signal is attached.

C, two chains working over pulleys at D, connected with the side frames of the target and dummy; their length regulated like the sash-cord of a window, so that when target A is at a sufficiently high point above the ground to be seen at the firing-point, B shall be at the bottom of the trench out of sight.

E E, sockets attached to sides of targets, working on guide-rods, F F, to secure correct vertical motion.

G, square-linked chain attached to cross-bar of dummy, working under and over pulleys H H, over a ratchet-wheel at I, and kept rigid by counterweights, K.

I, Ratchet-wheel with handle, to convey movement to target and dummy by means of chain G. When turned to the left, counterweight K is raised; target A, by its excess of weight over the dummy B, descends and raises B; and when turned to the right, B is brought down and A hauled up.

L, danger-signal fixed to an arm working on a centre, and provided with a counterbalance. When not required, the counterweight is hooked up to wire net on dummy.

WIMBLEDON TARGET. 55

PLATE 8.
The Wimbledon Target.

Elevation, showing the appearance of the target from the firing-point.

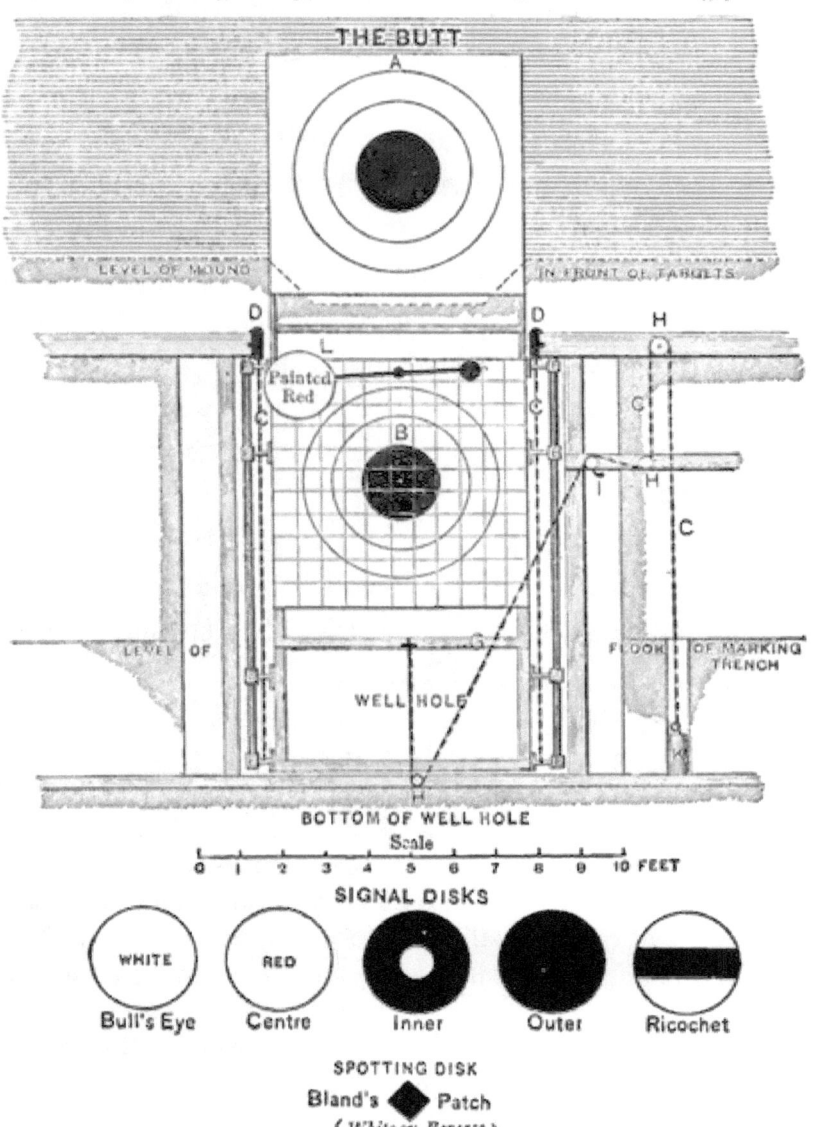

Signal-disks are suspended from the netting over the face of the dummy. They are used to show the *absolute* value of hits, and their approximate position. A separate disk is provided to show bull's-eyes, centres, inners, outers, and ricochets.

Each disk has a hook at the back, to admit of its being suspended from the wire netting stretched over the face of the dummy.

Spotting-disks.—A small diamond-shaped piece of zinc, painted white on one side and black on the other, with hook on each side.

The hook is placed in the actual shot-hole made, and the disk consequently shows the *exact* position of the hit.

Method of Working.—The target to be fired at is alone seen above the ground. The apparatus for working, sheltered by a parapet and trench, is out of sight, and protected from fire.

When a shot has struck the target, the marker in the trench proceeds as follows:

1. Unhooks the counterweight of the danger-signal, and thus allows the red disk to appear in view before the target.

2. Hooks on to the wire net stretched over the dummy that "signal-disk" which indicates the value of the hit, taking care to place such disk in as near a relative position as he can to the hit on the target.

3. Winds the ratchet-wheel in the direction which will lower the target A, and therefore raise the dummy B, with its signal-disk.

4. When A is lowered, he places, *in the actual shot-hole made*, a small zinc spotting-disk, with the white side to the front if the hit is on the bull's-eye, or the black side to the front if on white part of the target.

N. B.—The above applies to the first hit only. For the second, or any succeeding hits, when the target is lowered he moves the spotting-disk into the shot-hole last made, and covers over with patch paper the hole that the spotting-disk had previously covered.

5. Winds the ratchet-wheel in the direction to lower the dummy B, and raise the target A, for the next shot.

6. Removes the signal-disk from B, and waits for the next hit.

The above rules as to " spotting-disks " and " paper patches" apply to all systems of canvas targets where these articles are used.

BRUNEL'S TARGET.

The following plates show the plan of canvas target invented by Lieutenant-Colonel Brunel, and used by the Dominion of Canada Rifle Association at Ottawa.

PLATE 9.
Brunel's Target.
(SECTION.)

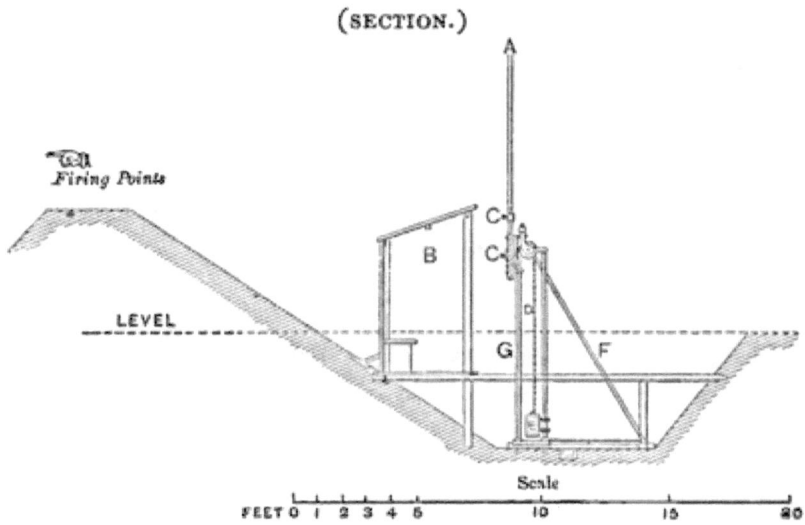

A, the target raised.
B, marker's hut.
C C, handles to move target.
D, chain connected to the target.
E, weight attached to other end of chain, balancing the target.
F, brace.
G, guide-rod.

EXPLANATION OF PLATE 10.

A, the target raised.
B B, braces.
C C, handles to move target.
D, chain connected to the target.
E, weight at other end of chain.
G G, iron guide-rods.

PLATE 10.
Brunel's Target.
(FRONT VIEW, TARGET RAISED.)

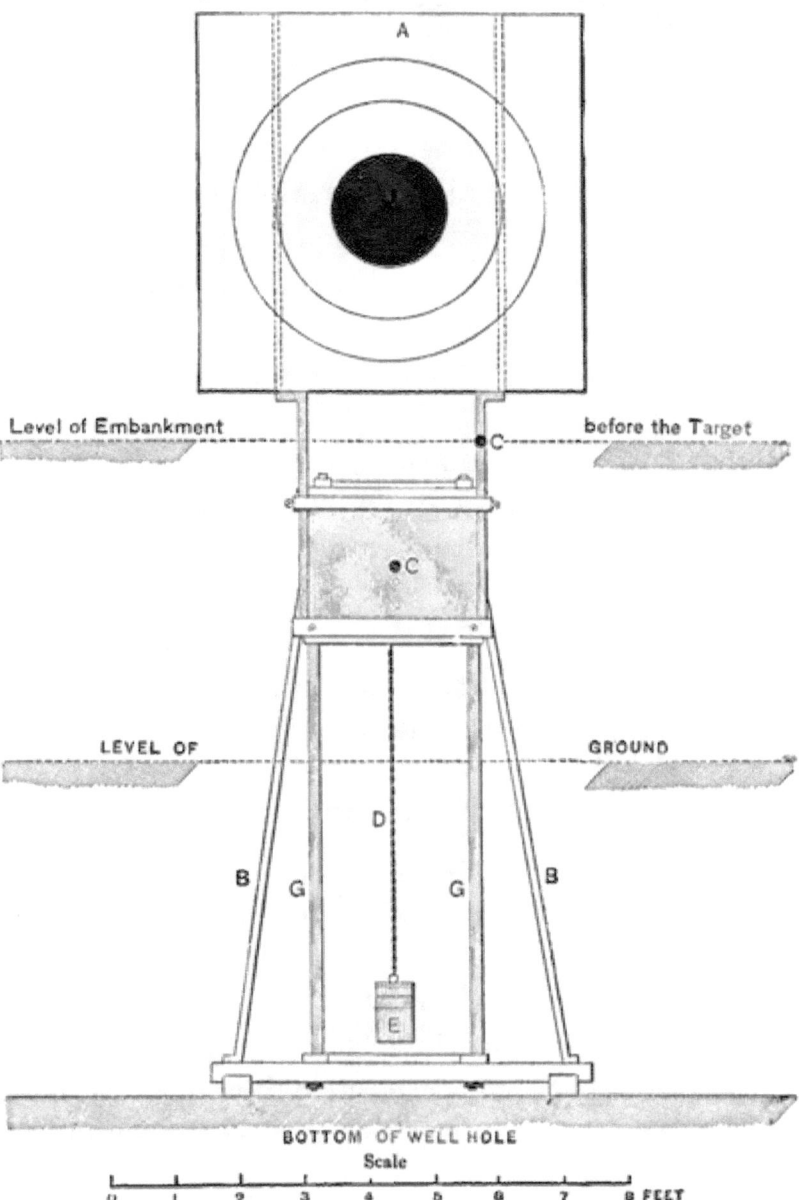

The target, A, is worked by the marker grasping the handles, C C, and drawing it down the iron guide-rods, G G, the counterbalancing weight, E, being proportionately drawn up by the process. The target then stands before the marker, who hangs in the bullet-hole (by means of a hook fastened at the back) a card-board disk, painted to indicate its value; lifts the handles, and raises the target to view again.

These disks will be shot through and through, but, when quite worn out, are cheaply replaced. At the next hit the marker repeats the process as above, taking the disk out of the first hole, patching that hole up, hanging a disk in the new hole, and again elevating the target.

The framework of the target is made of iron, sharpened at the front like a V, the lower sharp point or corner facing the firing-points.

SANFORD'S TARGET.

Lieutenant-Colonel E. Harrison Sanford, of New York, in 1877, designed a canvas target that should possess, in the main, all the principles and essentials of the Wimbledon target, but substituted for the mechanism of the latter a simpler construction, based largely upon the principle of a common window with upper and lower sashes, though, instead of balancing the sashes with separate weights, they were made to balance themselves, so that when one was pulled down, the other was simultaneously and proportionately raised.

The framework of this target is made of wood, and has two legs, which are secured to the sash by being pushed through staples fastened thereon.

By increasing or diminishing the length of these frames, any class target can be erected and changed at will by simply building the legs of the frame the same distance apart, so as to admit of their being passed through the staples and becoming an attachment of the sash. The canvas may be stretched over and tacked to the frame. Plates 11 and 12 illustrate the mechanism of the system, and show the dummy elevated above the level, and the target lowered into the pit.

The length of the pit must, of course, be sufficient to admit the target into it with, say, one foot margin each side.

Thus, if only second- and third-class targets are to be used, the pit should be about eight feet long by six feet wide at top, and seven feet deep.

A first-class target has been used in the diagram to show more plainly the manner of working.

PLATE 11.

Sanford's Target.

(SECTION.)

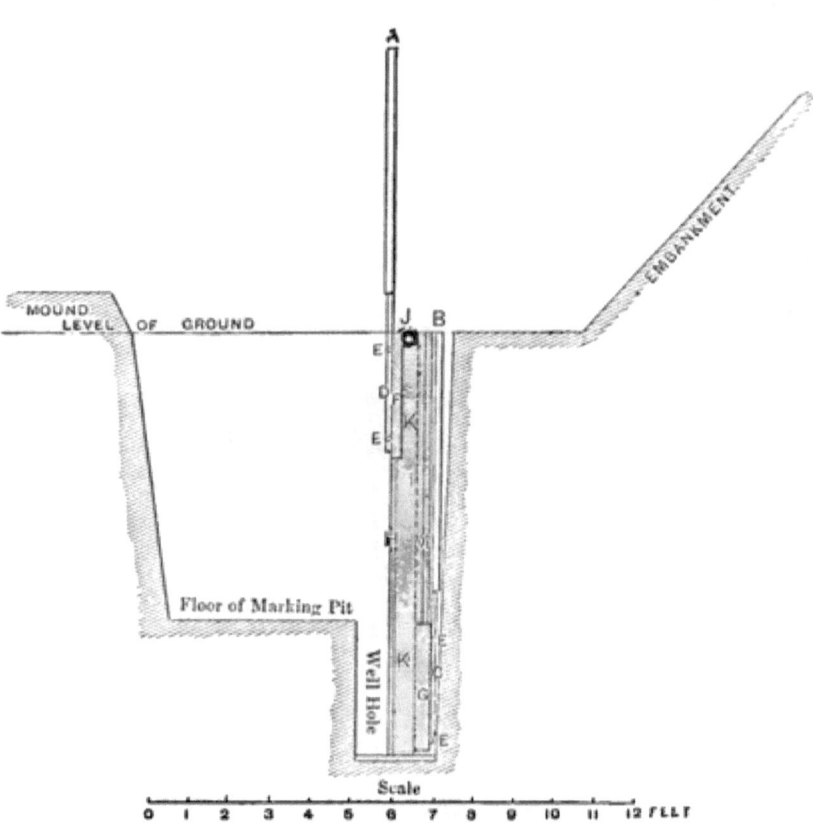

[For explanation, see page 64.]

PLATE 12.

Sanford's Target.

(FRONT VIEW OF DUMMY, TARGET, AND PIT.)

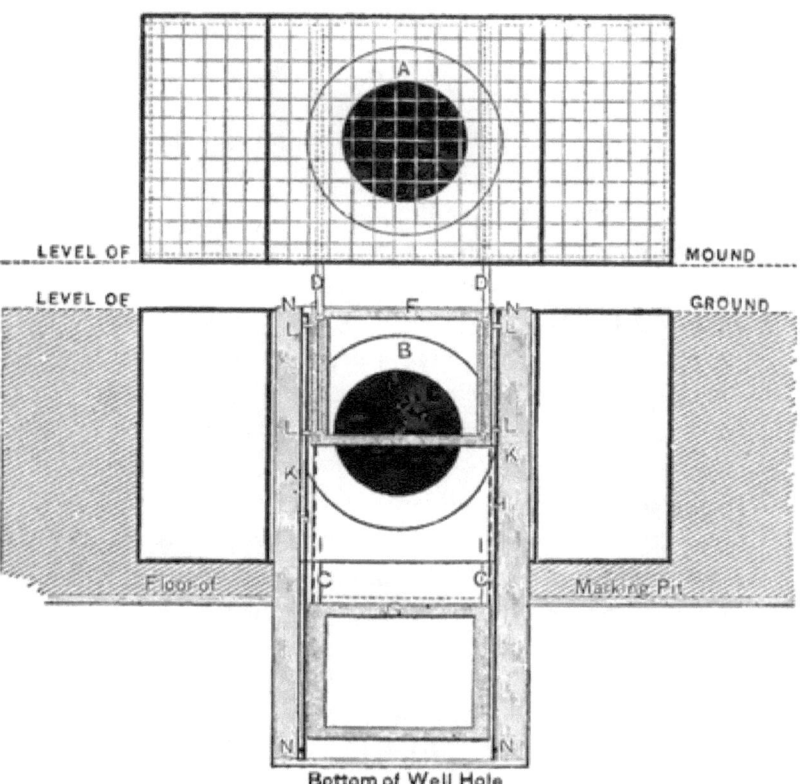

[For explanation, see page 64.]

Explanation of Plates 11 and 12 (pages 62, 63).

A, the dummy (covered with wire netting) raised.
B, the target lowered.
C, legs of target.
D, legs of dummy.
E, staples through which legs of target and dummy respectively slide.
F, framework sash supporting dummy.
G, framework sash supporting target.
H, iron guide-rods upon which sash of dummy works up and down at staples L L L L.
M, iron guide-rods (only one rod seen) upon which sash of target works similar to that of the dummy.
I, chains attached by a staple to top of the two sashes, and passing over the wheel J.
K K, wooden posts (to which are attached at N the guide-rods), securely braced together by horizontal timbers at top and bottom, in *front* of which the dummy, and *back* of which the target, passes on being moved up and down.
...., dotted lines on dummy show where framework extends. Same on the target.

The marking and signalling are done at this target in a similar manner to those of the Wimbledon Target, except as to the ricochet, when, instead of using a separate disk, the Creedmoor rule is observed of waving the red flag, or danger-signal, three times in front of the target.

DOUBLE TARGETS.

The preceding plan may be changed (perhaps advantageously where quick shooting is desired) by substituting in place of the dummy a second target, so that when a shot strikes the exposed target, the marker, upon locating it, raises the disk denoting its value, and, placing it over the hole, allows it to remain in view for a few seconds, after which he lowers that target (the second one being thereupon raised and exposed), patches the bullet-hole, and repeats as soon as the other target is struck.

SWINGING TARGETS.

The following diagrams show a system of canvas targets in use upon a Range in New Jersey. The firing-points are all on one line, the targets being erected as many yards distant from the firing-points as desired. With this plan a series of "stone fences," iron mantlets, or protection for markers, is required, *one fence* sheltering the markers of *two targets*.

This can best be explained by the following illustration:

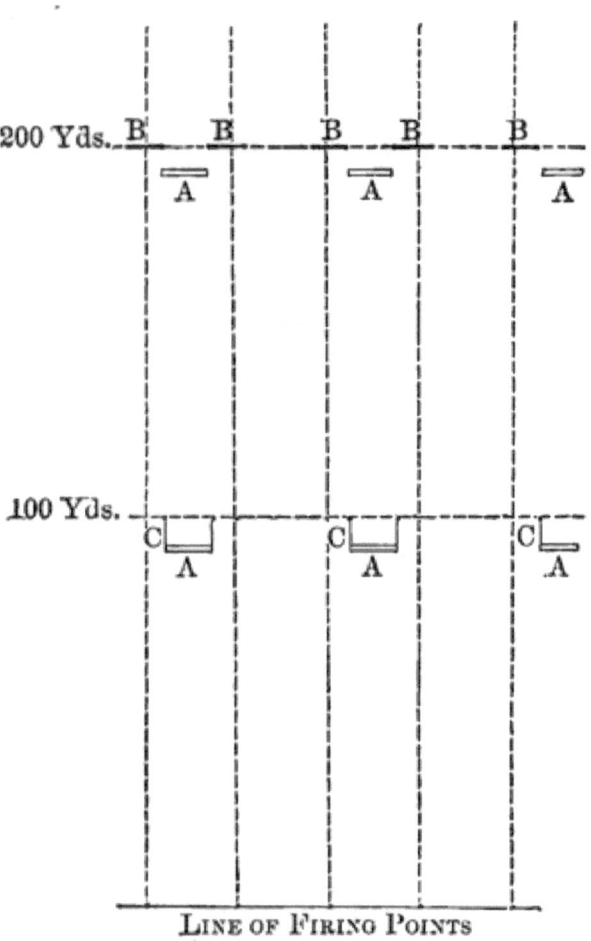

A, the marker's fence or protection.
B, the targets swung open, or exposed.
C, the targets closed, or swung in.

PLATE 13.

Swinging Targets,

Used upon a Range in New Jersey.

(As seen from the firing-points.)

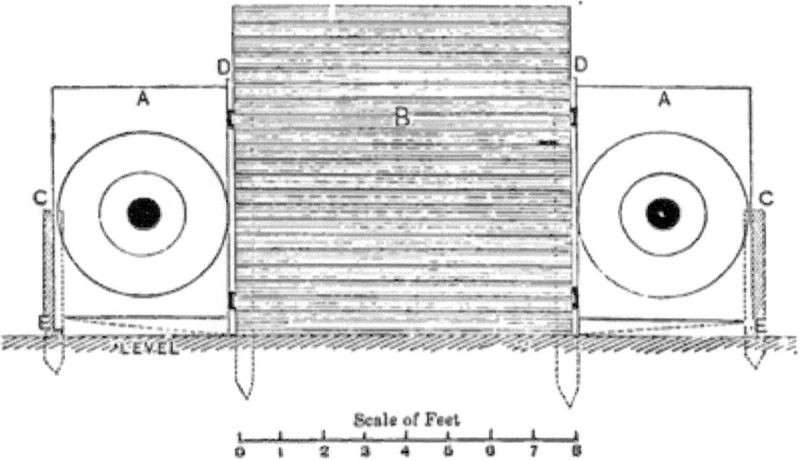

A A, the targets open, or exposed.

B, fence or protection behind which markers stand, painted black.

C C, posts to prevent targets from *swinging back* too far, strongly braced.

D D, posts upon which targets are hinged. (These posts are as many feet back from the fence as the target measures across its face; thus, with third-class targets as above, they are a little over 4 feet in rear of the fence; if a second-class target, they would be placed 6 feet from the fence, and 12 feet for a first-class target.)

E E shows where a pulley is fastened to a post through which an endless rope runs. This rope is attached to the lower left and right corners of the respective targets; and the marker, by pulling one side of the rope, *draws the target to him*, or shut, and by pulling the other, *draws the target from him*, or open.

The framework of these targets is made of pine-wood, 1 inch thick, 3 inches wide, and braced at the back to prevent the target from sagging. The canvas is nailed on this framework, and marking is done by pulling in the target, and hanging in the bullet-hole a small black or white disk, and, upon the target being pushed open again, the marker puts forth a disk over the spot struck indicating its value. At the next shot he closes the target again, takes the small disk out of bullet-hole previously made, patches that hole, hangs the small disk in the new hole, and marks as above.

JEWELL'S TARGET.

Still another canvas target of recent invention is that commonly known as "Jewell's Target." It was experimented with at Creedmoor, but the existing prejudice against canvas compelled its removal.

Major Herbert S. Jewell, of Brooklyn, N. Y., kindly furnished the writer with diagrams from which the following reduced illustrations have been taken.

They show a left-handed target; but to change to right-hand, if desired, it will only be necessary to make a transposition from one side to the other.

PLATE 14.
Jewell's Target.
(FRONT ELEVATION.)

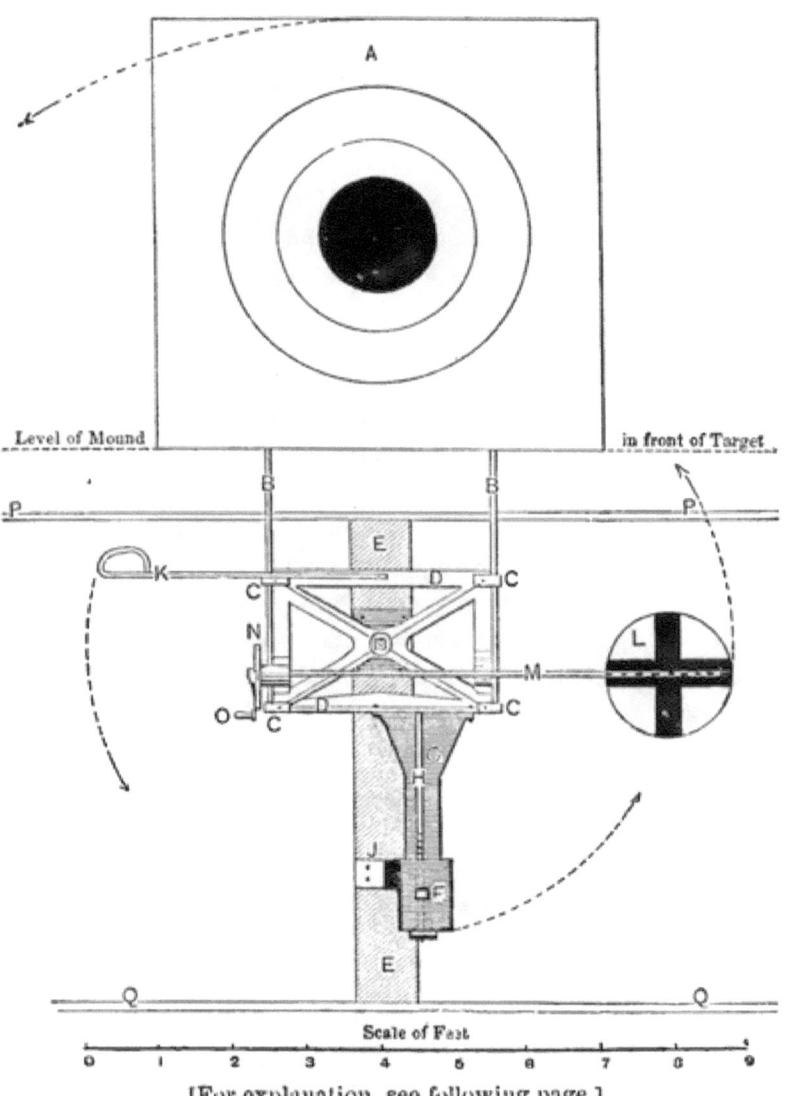

[For explanation, see following page.]

Explanation of Plate 14.

A, the target raised.

B B, legs of target passing through

C C C C, iron sockets.

D, a framework supporting the target, and working upon a centre-pin or spindle (12 inches long) securely fastened to

E, a heavy timber at back of pit.

F, a weight counterbalancing the target, which can be raised or lowered according to weight desired.

G, iron arm holding weight to framework, D.

H, iron feather on arm, with notches for the purpose of raising or lowering the counterbalance weight. The weight is held in place by a set screw tapped into the weight, the point of which is screwed into the desired notch.

J, iron stop with rubber tip, preventing target from revolving too far, and against which weight rests when target is elevated.

K, iron lever with handle firmly secured to upper part of framework.

L, signalling disk or disks (explained in Fig. 3).

M, rod of same, connecting with

N, a notched stationary wheel (explained in Fig. 2).

O, handle of notched wheel.

P, level of ground and top of pit.

Q, floor of pit.

The mechanism permits of any class target being used by taking out the frame and legs of one target and substituting another. The pit must, however, be made sufficiently long and deep to admit of the drawing-down of the largest-size target to be used. The framework and machinery are all made of iron, but the writer inclines to the belief that woodwork should be substituted where practicable, thus making the whole mechanism less cumbersome.

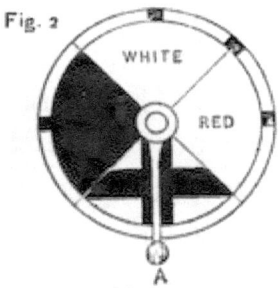

A, the handle.

Fig. 2 represents N on Plate 14. It is a stationary iron wheel, about 10 inches in diameter, the handle only turning. It has five notches, into either of which the spring-arm of the handle may be placed. Four notches are in the centre of the divided quarters, painted as shown above, and signify respectively bull's-eye, centre, inner, and outer; the other notch is on the line between the red and white quarters, and signals a ricochet, the disk presenting to view one side red and the other white.

The handle is attached to the rod (M on Plate 14), at the other end of which is a disk (L), designed and painted to signal any of the five signals of bull's-eye, centre, inner, outer, and ricochet.

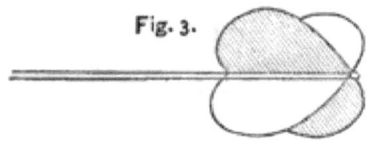
Fig. 3.

Fig. 3 explains its formation. Each disk is *round*, and is modelled upon the principle of a revolving railroad switch-signal. It will now be understood that by turning the handle of the "notched wheel," the disk at the other extremity of the rod is correspondingly turned. As shown above, the handle is in the "inner" notch, the "inner" disk being turned to the front by the process.

SYSTEM OF MARKING.

When a shot strikes the target, the marker sees, and mentally locates, the value of the shot, turns the handle connecting with the revolving disk into the desired notch, grasps the lever, and pulls the target over (he is provided with two small disks made of wood, tin, or iron, with a hook in centre and each side of them, and painted respectively white and red, and black cross and black), hangs the disk denoting value in the shot-hole, patches the last hole, lifts the lever, and swings the target into position ready for the next shot.

THE REVOLVING TARGET.

A target of cheap and simple construction, known as the "Revolving Target," designed by General George W. Wingate, the General Inspector of Rifle Practice, State of New York, is used to some extent by the United States Army and others, and gives general satisfaction.

A pit is first dug 13 or 14 feet long by 7 or 8 feet deep and about 6 feet wide for targets of the third class, and proportionately deeper and longer for targets of the second and first classes.

A stout upright post or beam is driven into the ground and firmly braced, its upper end being level with the top of the pit. An iron pin is then fastened, so as to project from this upright post, forming the axis upon which the target revolves.

The framework of two targets is connected by a cross-piece, through the centre or hub of which the iron pin or pivot passes, and the targets revolve upon it on the principle of a wheel.

PLATE 15.
Revolving Targets.
(SECTION OF TARGETS AND PIT.)

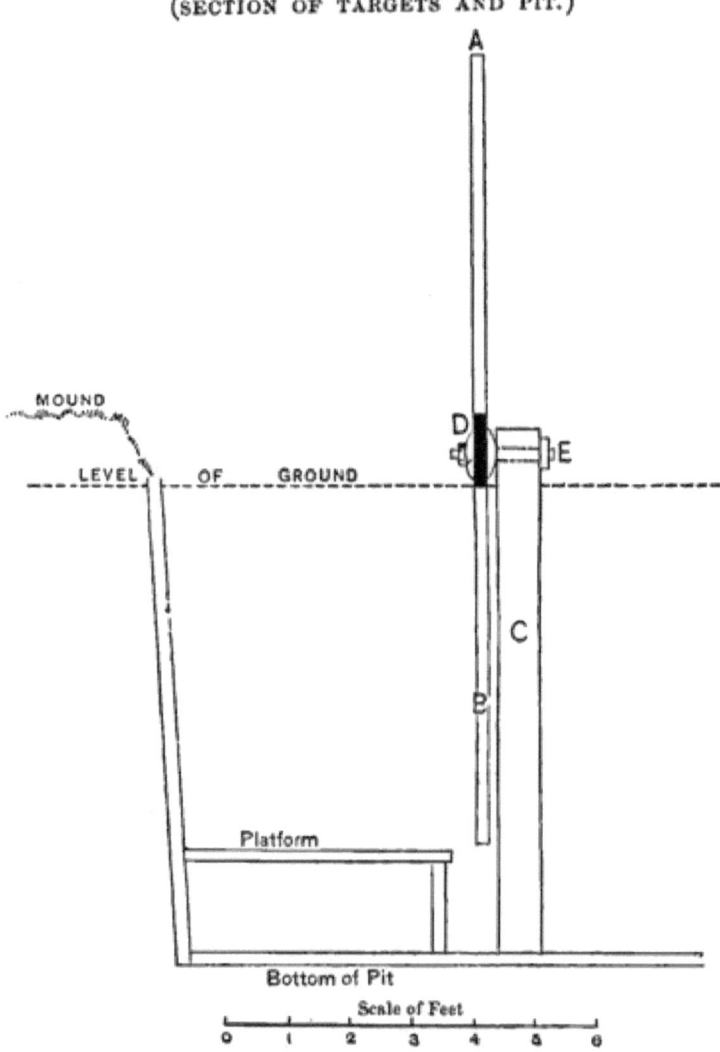

A, target exposed.
B, other target in the pit.
C, upright post holding targets.
D, the hub in centre of framework connecting the two targets.
E, iron pin on which hub turns.

PLATE 16.
Revolving Targets.
(FRONT VIEW OF TARGETS AND PIT.)

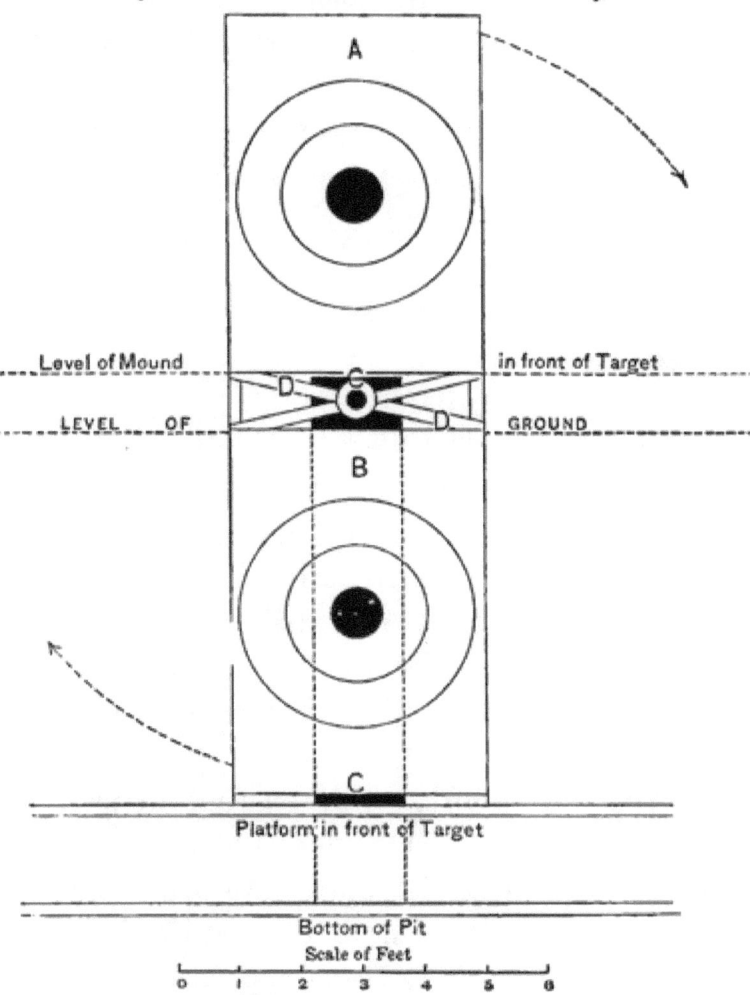

A, target exposed.
B, other target in the pit.
C C, upright post holding the targets upon central pin.
D D, framework with hub in centre.

System of Marking.—When the exposed target is struck, the marker raises a disk denoting the value of the shot, and places it for an instant over the bullet-hole in the target hit; he then, with his right hand, pushes the other target to the left and up to the perpendicular, patches the shot-hole just made in target No. 1, and is ready to repeat as soon as target No. 2 is struck.

The following, which for want of a better name is here called

THE "POSSIBLE" TARGET,

was devised not long since, but has never, to the author's knowledge, been publicly used. For simplicity of action and construction it appears to possess merit, and it is claimed that the marking can be very prompt in the hands of a skilful man. The firing-points for all distances can be established on the one line, as, when not in use, the target can be drawn down flat, a few inches below the level of the ground, and so not interfere with the view of objects beyond. As with the iron targets, a pit must be dug at the required distance from the firing-point $6\frac{1}{4}$ feet deep, 8 feet long (for second- or third-class targets, and about 14 feet long for first-class), and 9 feet wide (north and south) at its extreme width, as shown in the following diagrams. The canvas is tightly stretched upon a framework of angular iron, and works like a *lid* to the pit, hinging upon a solid wooden roller, being opened and shut at will, the weight of the target being counterbalanced by weights suspended under the roller. If found necessary, the distance between the weights and the roller can be increased, and more leverage thus obtained in raising and lowering the target. It will be noticed on Plate 17 at B, and on Plate 18 at C C—the "continuation of iron framework," etc.—that that portion of the framework has a "shoulder" which rests upon the upper part of the roller, and permits of its being securely and tightly screwed by the key or nut underneath.

PLATE 17.

(SECTION.)

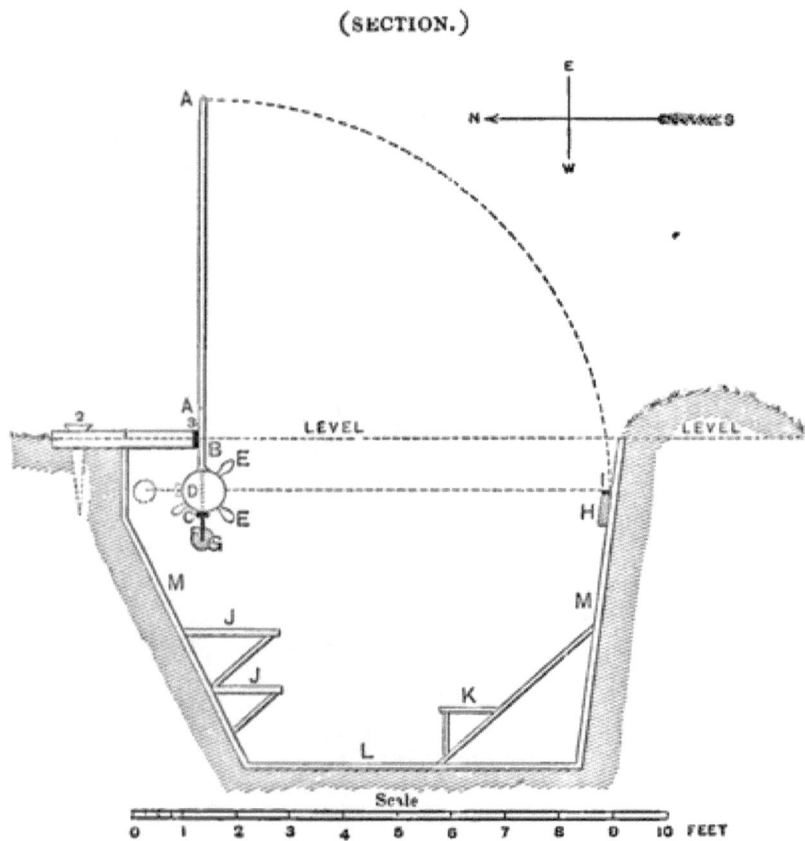

Explanation of Plate 17.

A to A, angular iron framework of target.
B, continuation of iron framework passing through the wooden roller, D, and screwed tight by
C, the key or nut.
D, the wooden roller.
E E, wooden handles to turn the roller.
F, iron rod under roller bearing weights.
G, the weights (iron or lead).
H, wood supporting top of target when pulled down.
I, thick rubber on top of wood.
J J, marker's shelves for holding paste, patches, disks, etc.
K, marker's seat to be placed against left side of pit.
L, floor of pit.
M M, walls of pit.
1, a piece of timber fastened in the ground by
2, a wooden spike or spikes, and tipped at the end by
3, a piece of thick rubber.

80   THE RIFLE CLUB AND RANGE.

PLATE 18.

(FRONT ELEVATION.)

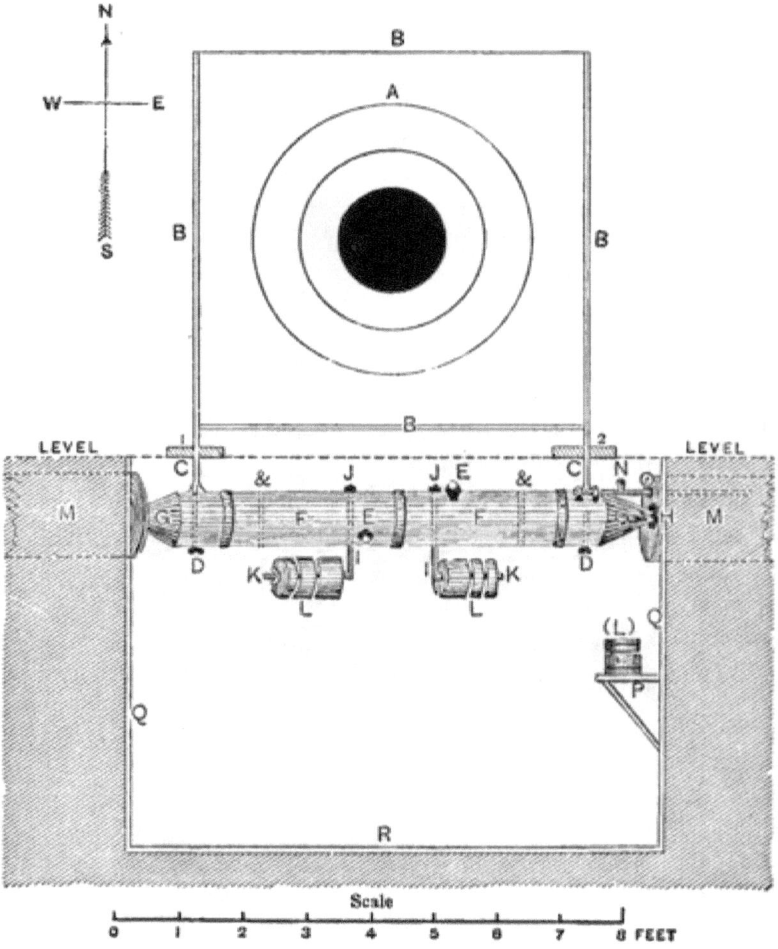

Explanation of Plate 18.

A, the target.

B B B B, the angular iron frame upon which target is stretched.

C C, continuation of frame through roller, F, secured by

D D, keys or nuts.

E E, handles by which roller is turned.

F F, the wooden roller.

G G, iron tips to roller working in

H, an iron socket (same both ends).

I I, iron rods bearing the weights to balance target, and passing through the roller, F, secured at the top by

J J, iron nuts.

K K, continuation of iron rod bearing weights with key or nut to keep

L L, the weights, in their place.

(L), spare weights.

M M, timber laid solid in ground holding the attached iron sockets in which the iron tips (G G) of the roller work. (A portion of the trunk of a tree is best for this purpose.)

N, an iron bolt used in case of a strong north wind to keep target from blowing forward; must, of course, be unbolted every time the target is marked, or a wheel with teeth might be used instead.

O, iron-bound hole in M, in which bolt works.

P, table holding extra weights.

Q, side-walls of pit.

R, floor of pit.

1, 2, timbers, tipped with rubber, keeping target from falling backward with a south wind.

& &, holes through roller ready for the third-class target to be fastened as above.

REDUCED TARGETS,

or the N. R. A. target reduced in size proportionately to distance, are much used for indoor practice; and, though not affording an absolutely accurate comparison of scores made upon the Range (where wind, weather, light, and atmosphere have to be considered), they are of considerable value as a means of approximate comparison.

Reduced paper targets are regularly manufactured, and may be purchased ready for use. They can, however, be easily made by following a simple rule of scaling. Thus, if the bull's-eye of the regular third-class target at 200 yards measures 8 inches in diameter, and it is desired to shoot at a distance of 25 yards, or 75 feet, at the same target reduced to make the distance equal to 200 yards, it is only necessary to calculate as follows: bull's-eye at 200 yards is 8 inches in diameter; at 100 yards it is 4 inches; at 50 yards it is 2 inches; at 25 yards it is 1 inch, and so on with the other divisions of the target. These rules will, of course, apply to any class target, and need no other explanation.

BRINTON RIFLE RANGE.

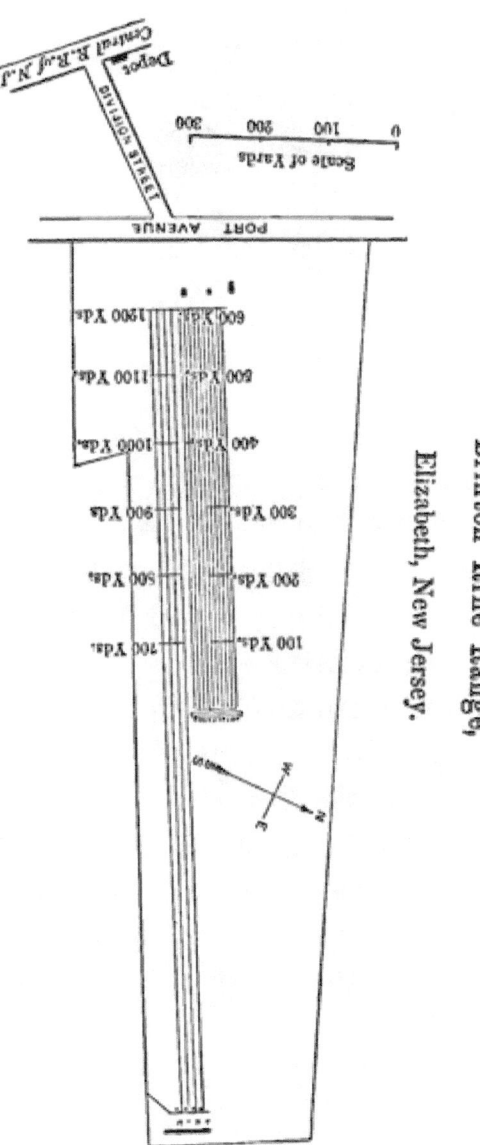

Marking-disks.

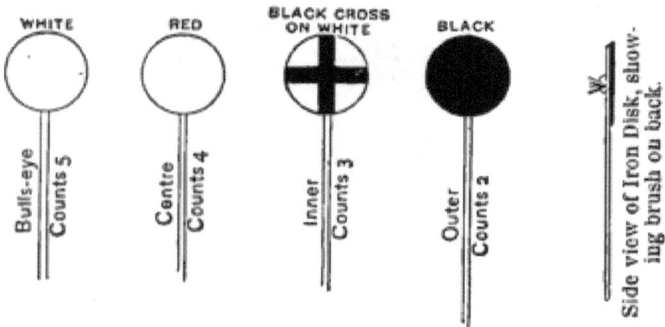

MARKING-DISKS ADOPTED BY THE NATIONAL RIFLE ASSOCIATION OF AMERICA.

The disks used at second- and third-class targets are usually 18 inches in diameter, while those used at the first-class targets are about 30 inches in diameter. The poles in use at Creedmoor are about 8 feet in length. For iron targets, sheet or galvanized iron disks are the most durable. For canvas or other targets, where no brush is required at the back, they may be made of iron, wood, tin, canvas stretched upon a hoop, or strong card-board, each arranged with either a handle or hook, as required.

For canvas targets, the spotting-disk to be hung in the bullet-hole may be made of iron, tin, or card-board, and may be round or square, as fancy dictates, having a hook in the centre. White is required for spotting a shot on the bull's-eye, and black for any other portion of the target.

PAPER PATCHES

for canvas, wood, or paper targets. Plenty of these should be provided for each target, and may be pasted on with common paste at time of covering hole, or may be gummed beforehand, requiring only to be moistened to make them adhere. They should be white and black, so as not to deface the target, and should be cut round, 2 or 3 inches in diameter.

DANGER-SIGNALS

for the firing-points should be flags made of red bunting about 2 × 3 feet in size, the edges all hemmed and fastened to poles 12 or 14 feet high, pointed and tipped with iron at the bottom, to allow of their being stuck in the ground.

At the targets (as bunting is expensive and easily torn) danger-signals of tin, iron, canvas, or wood painted red may be made and fastened to a pole like the disk; but the danger-signal should be *much larger* than, and of a *different shape* from, the disk, or else it might easily be mistaken at a distance for a "centre."

TRIGGER-TESTERS.

These are indispensable to test the triggers of rifles, according to the Regulations of the National Rifle Association, which require "military" rifles to sustain upon the trigger, full cocked, the minimum weight of 6 lbs., and "any" rifles 3 lbs.

They are easily made by attaching to a rod of iron, bent to an angle or hook at the upper end (to hang on the trigger), as much lead as will, with rod and all, weigh respectively 3 and 6 lbs.

WIND-INDICATORS,

or contrivances to show plainly from which direction the wind blows, are most easily and readily obtained by using flags or streamers, or both, for such purpose.

They should be fastened to poles from 20 to 40 feet high, and erected on the embankment or fence in rear of the targets, as well as at regular distances along the side or sides of the Range. Red bunting is most generally used, though other colors are sometimes substituted. Streamers are better indicators than flags.

A common wind-vane will be of some benefit to marksmen in determining the direction of the wind, but the addition of a clock-dial will be of great assistance.

PLATE 19.
Dial Wind-indicator.

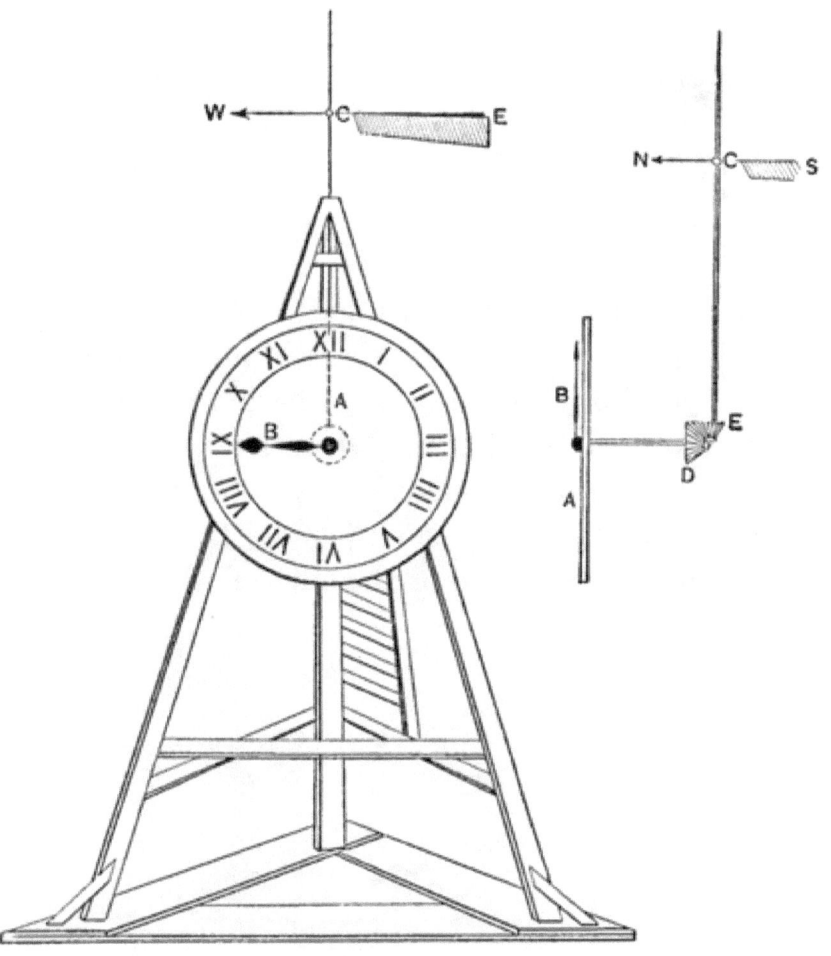

Explanation of Plate 19.

A, face of the dial.
B, the hand.
C, the wind-vane.
D, cog-wheel of hand turned by
E, cog-wheel of wind-vane.

The face can be made of wood or iron, any size, and placed as high as desired.

When the wind-vane is true north, place the hand at XII and connect the cog-wheel, and the instrument is set. As shown above, it is a "nine-o'clock," or west, wind.

Though the erection of many wind-indicators is desirable, their use in numbers is not imperative, except at the longer ranges, where nicer calculations have to be made. One or two streamers should certainly be placed upon the top of the embankment, and, say, one flag or streamer every two hundred yards along the side of the Range.

Massachusetts Rifle Association.
Diagram of Range, Walnut Hill, Mass. (9 miles from Boston).

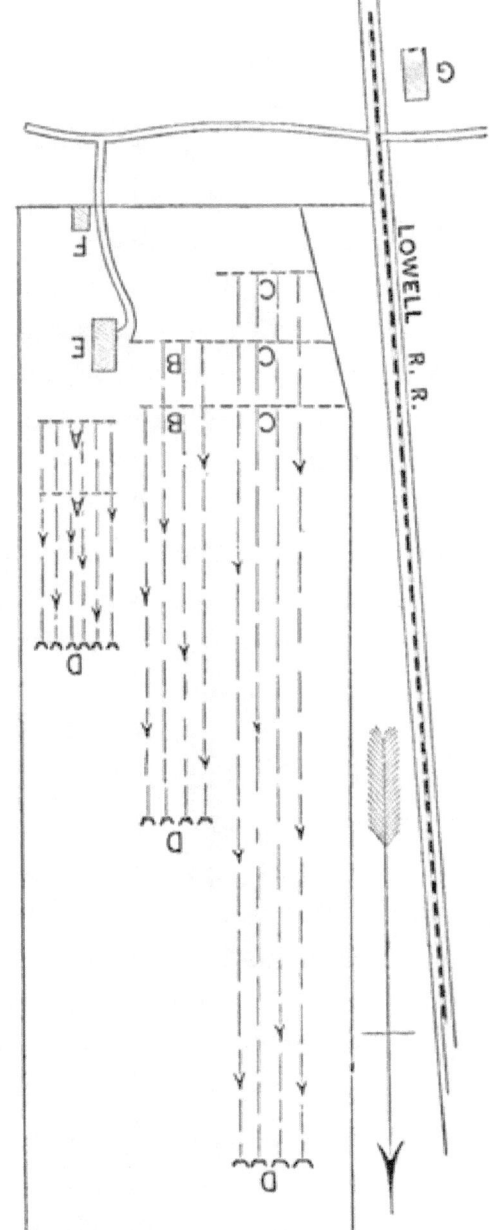

G, Walnut Hill Station.
A A, short-range firing-points.
B B, mid-range firing-points.
C C C, long-range firing-points.
D D D, targets.
E, office of M. R. A.

SCORING-BOARDS.

Though not essential, these boards are decidedly useful, and facilitate the duties of the score-keeper by holding the tickets of competitors at his target constantly before him.

They should be made of tin, about a foot in length, and of a uniform width, the side edges being bent over to form a groove, into which the score tickets may slide.

Having now seen some of the numerous designs of targets and appurtenances, we will shout "Excelsior!" and suppose our newly formed Association to have secured its Range, and erected, say, six targets, which can be changed at will to first, second, or third class. The Range is equipped and ready for active service. It is the spring of the year, and the opening of the Range has been decided to take place on, say, the 15th of May. Our Prize Committee has been, and still is, hard at work obtaining donations of prizes. Our Board of Directors, or Executive Committee, in conjunction with the Prize Committee, meets about a month, or at least three weeks, prior to the opening day; and, having received a full report to date from the Prize Committee, decides upon a programme as follows:

PROGRAMME OF SPRING MEETING

AND

Opening of the Range of —— —— Rifle Association,

TO BE HELD AT —— RANGE,

ON WEDNESDAY, MAY 15, 18—, COMMENCING AT 9 O'CLOCK A.M.

Competition No. 1, May 15, at 9 A.M.

"DIRECTORS' MATCH."

Open only to Directors and Honorary Directors of the —— —— Rifle Association. Distance, 200 yards. Position, standing. Five shots. Any rifle. Entrance-fee, $1.

PRIZE.

The Directors' championship gold badge, provided by the Directors themselves, to be shot for annually, and held by the winner during the year; value $50.

Competition No. 2, May 15.

"SHORT-RANGE MATCH."

(Limited to 100 Entries.)

Open to all comers. Distance, 200 yards. Seven shots. Position, standing. Weapon, any military rifle. Entrance-fee, $1.

PRIZES.

1st Prize,	a —— rifle, presented by ——, of ——; value....	$100
2d "	a gold medal, presented by ——, of ——; value....	50
3d "	a silver cup, presented by ——, of ——; value $25, and cash $5........................	30
4th "	20% of the total entrance-fees.	
5th "	15% " " "	
6th "	10% " " "	

Six Prizes.

Competition No. 3, May 15.

"Team Match."

(Entries limited to 15 Teams.)

Open to teams of four men from any regularly organized Rifle Club, or Association, or Military Organization. If the latter, to appear in the uniform of their corps. Members of teams to have been regularly enlisted, or elected members of the organization represented, and to have been such for at least one month prior to the day upon which this match is announced to be shot. Distances, 200 and 500 yards, seven shots at each distance. Weapon: in the case of teams representing military organizations, the rifle with which they are uniformly armed; in other cases, any military rifle, excluding specials. Entrance-fee, $5 each team.

PRIZES.

1st. To the team making the highest aggregate score, a trophy, value.. $100
2d. To the team making the second highest aggregate score, a silver cup, presented by ——, of ——, value $25; and a club or regimental pin to each member of the team, value $25.................................. 50
3d. A bronze medal, value $15, and cash $10.............. 25

Three Prizes. Total value..... ..... $175

Competition No. 4, May 15.

"Consolation Match."

(Limited to 80 Entries.)

Open only to those who have not won any individual prize during this meeting. Distance, 500 yards. Seven shots. Weapon, any rifle. Position, any. Entrance-fee, $1.

PRIZES.

1st.	A silver urn, presented by ——, of ——; value.........	$50
2d.	A life membership in this Association, value ——, and cash ——.	35
3d.	A —— military rifle, presented by ——, of ——; value.	20
4th.	Cash...	10
5th.	Cash...	9
	Five Prizes. Total value............	$124

Competition No. 5, May 16.
"Long-range Match."

Open to all comers. Distances, 800, 900, and 1000 yards. Fifteen shots at each distance. Position, any. Entrance-fee, $1. No coaching allowed.

PRIZES.

1st. A —— Creedmoor rifle, presented by ——, of ——; value .... $——

2d. A life membership in this Association, value ——, and cash —— .... ——

3d. 15% of total entrance-fees.

4th. 10% of total entrance-fees.

Four Prizes.

TIME TABLE.

Trains leave, etc.   Boats, etc.

Refreshments on the ground at reasonable rates.

Admission at gate, 50 cents to all non-members.

General Rules.

No sighting shots will be allowed in any match, but Pool Targets will be open continuously at distances to correspond with the matches in progress. Tickets good for one shot at any Pool Target will be sold at the Headquarters Tent upon the Range at 10 cents each. Fifty per cent. of the gross pool receipts will be divided *pro rata* among those making *bull's-eyes* at the Pool Targets (who will be furnished with a ticket upon making a bull's-eye).

Entries to matches must be made either in person or by letter to the Secretary, at his office, No. —— —— Street, on or before May 10 next. Entries received after that date will be charged 50 *per cent. extra* as *Post Entries*, and must take their chances of target accommodation. No entry will be received unless accompanied by the amount of entry charges, either in cash or in post-office or money order for value.

Please fill out, sign, and forward enclosed entry blank in accordance with the following.

—— ——,
Secretary.

FORM OF ENTRY BLANK.

To be filled up by competitor or team and returned to the Secretary, ———— ————, on or before May 10, 18—.

☞ Write the word "*this*" opposite match entered for. ☜

Individual Matches, May 15, 18—.

Competition.	Match.	Yards.	Rifle.	Open to	Write "*This*" here.	Amount Enclosed.	Leave these columns blank.		No.
							Hour.	Target.	
1	Directors'.	200	Any.	Directors.		$ c.			
2	Short Range.	200	Any Mil.	All comers.					
4	Consolation.	500	Any.	See Progr.					
5	Long Range.	{ 800 900 1000 }	Any.	All comers.	May 16.				

Total, $ ....

Name, ...

Address, ...
....

Team Match, May 15, 18—.

Competition.	Match.	Yards.	Rifle.	Open to	Write "*This*" here.	Amount Enclosed.	Leave these columns blank.		No.
							Hour.	Target.	
3	Team.	{ 200 500 }	See Progr.	Teams of 5.		$ c.			

Organization, ...

Team Captain, ...

Address, ...

Total, $ .... enclosed.

Write plainly, and enclose stamps for return of tickets if desired. If they are not received in time, apply on Range.

The preceding is our programme complete. It should be the Secretary's duty to see that the same is correctly printed, and afterwards distributed. A good form for a programme, and one that has received universal favor, is that of printing it on two, four, or more pages, of a medium size, each page, say, $5\frac{1}{2}$ by 3 inches, made to fold like a little book or pamphlet. This is convenient alike for reference and carrying.

The great aim in inaugurating our first Prize Meeting should be not so much to make it pay as not to lose by it; though even if some pecuniary loss should appear, it will be fully covered—if not too large—by the future good results and publicity of our opening.

It is a bold stroke to pretend to show anything like the receipts and expenses of conducting this Spring Meeting, when it is not known to whom or where it may apply; but we will suppose an instance of average enterprise and discretion on the part of the management, a reasonable number of riflemen, fair weather, and with the matches announced, admission to the Range 50 cents each to non-members, and 25 cents extra for each saddle-horse or horse and wagon, and estimate how we shall stand.

EXPENSES.

For printing 2000 4-page Programmes of Meeting.						$10 00		
"	"	2000 Entrance Blanks.............					5 00	
"	"	25 Entrance or Score Tickets, Match 1.						
"	"	150	"	"	"	"	2.	
"	"	25	"	"	"	"	3.	
"	"	100	"	"	"	"	4.	
"	"	75	"	"	"	"	5.	
"	"	375	"	"	"	....	10 00	
"	"	500 Admission Tickets to Range....					3 00	
"	"	500 Pool Tickets....................					3 00	
"	"	500 Bull's-eye Tickets.............					3 00	
"	"	500 Competitors' Number Tickets (Individual) and 75 Competitors' Number Tickets (Team)........					3 00	37 00

PRIZES.

3d Prize, Match No. 2..........................	5 00	
1st Prize, Match No. 3..........................	100 00	
2d Prize, Match No. 3, Pins or Medals..........	25 00	
3d Prize, Match No. 3, Medal and Cash.........	25 00	
Match No. 4, Cash.............................	19 00	174 00

ON RANGE.

1st day, 6 Scorers @ $2........................	12 00	
1st day, 6 Markers @ $1 25....................	7 50	
2d day, 4 Scorers @ $2..........................	8 00	
2d day, 4 Markers @ $1 25.....................	5 00	32 50
Total Expenses for Meeting......................	$243 50	

RECEIPTS.

Ent.-fees, Match 1, 15 @ $1				$15 00
Ent.-fees, Match 2, 90 @ $1	$90 00			
" " 2, 10 @ $1 50	15 00	$105 00		
Less divisions of money, 20%	21 00			
" " " 15%	15 75			
" " " 10%	10 50	47 25	57 75	
Ent.-fees, Match 3, 12 teams @ $5			60 00	
Ent.-fees, Match 4, 75 @ $1			75 00	
Ent.-fees, Match 5, 20 @ $1	20 00			
" " 5 @ $1 50	7 50	27 50		
Less divisions of money, 15%	4 12			
" " " 10%	2 75	6 87	20 63	$228 38
Sold 500 Pool Tickets @ 10c	50 00			
Less paid Bull's-eyes	25 00			25 00
Admissions at Gate				75 00
				$328 38
Expenses				243 50
Balance				$84 88

This balance will be used up for sundries, postage, lunch, etc., so that, though showing no large balance of money, we make our Spring Meeting an event of interest to riflemen, we advertise our existence, we secure members, we show what we can do, and, last but not least, we establish our association and give it this gratifying start, and all without losing one cent; and the chances are that by judicious advertising beforehand, and with the aid of a *live* Prize Committee, we can both increase the number of our donated prizes and also the number of competitors and spectators, and so correspondingly increase the balance in our treasury. And here let it be borne in mind that great care should be taken in the selection of the Annual Prize Committee, the most active and influential members only being appointed as members thereof.

For some time previous to the adoption and issue of the programme, let *every member* of the Board of Directors consider himself a member *pro tem.* of this committee, and use his personal exertions to obtain prizes, reporting promptly to the Prize Committee proper every donation so obtained. It is a comparatively unappreciated fact that more responsibility indirectly rests upon this committee for the success of a meeting than upon any other committee or officer, not only in the obtaining of prizes, but also in the placing of them so as to be appropriate and attractive.

It is also a very slowly appreciated fact in this country that the *desires of the competitors should be ascertained* regarding the *kind of prizes* that will be acceptable. In Europe more diversity exists, the donations of articles foreign to rifle-shooting being as eagerly sought after as the other class. It is no uncommon occurrence to find in the programmes of European and other foreign rifle associations such prizes as orders for wearing-apparel, musical instruments, sewing-machines, smoker's articles, provisions, jewelry, etc. The "rifle pulse" should likewise be carefully felt as to offering *money* prizes.

The foregoing programme has been printed in detail, not so much with the intention of its being made a criterion as to matches, conditions, and prizes (which can only be arranged by those knowing the circumstances and wants of the particular classes and numbers likely to visit and patronize the Range), but more to show the form and general style, and, most of all, to make a basis upon which to understandingly work out the practical management and "running" of the matches, entries, etc.

Having, therefore, shown the financial probabilities and possibilities of successfully carrying out our programme, we will next go on and familiarize ourselves with the practical internal workings of the different departments, commencing with the

SECRETARY'S DEPARTMENT.

Immediately upon the adoption of the programme, the Secretary should consult with the Executive Officer as to the probable number of entries in each match, and having agreed upon a maximum, at least twenty per cent. over that number of score tickets should be printed.

First, for "Competition No. 1, Directors' Match," score cards similar to Plate No. 1 (in "Forms of Score Cards," pp. 135–144) should be printed; for "Competition No. 2, Short-range Match," Plate No. 2; for "Competition No. 3, Team Match," Plate No. 3; for "Competition No. 4, Consolation Match," Plate No. 4; and for "Competition No. 5, Long-range Match," score cards as shown in Plate No. 5.

The printer should be instructed to print score tickets on card-board of medium thickness, and *color for distance*, i. e., one color for each distance in all matches; or, plainer still, say, all tickets for 200 yards, *white;* tickets for 500 yards, *yellow;* for 800 yards, *pink;* for 900 yards, *green;* for

1000 yards, *blue*, etc. Have them printed on tints rather than positive colors. This rule of "color for distance" prevents the possibility of a competitor shooting upon a 500-yard ticket at 200 yards, and *vice versa*, as the scorekeeper is made familiar with the color corresponding to each distance.

Every score ticket must be numbered on the back (on ticket and coupon) from No. 1 up to as many numbers as there are tickets at *each distance* and *each match*. These numbers may be printed or written. They are used only for the purpose of comparing a detached coupon with the original ticket in case of dispute, and have no other significance.

The "Competitor's Number" must next be attended to, and should be printed on light cardboard as follows:

The same form will do for teams by substituting the word "Team" for "Competitor" wherever it occurs, and correcting the phraseology to conform to the change. The numbers in the square may be printed or written, and should be from one up to, and somewhat in excess of, as many individuals or teams as are expected to compete in all of the matches, one ticket and number for *each* individual and team. To readily distinguish the two classes, the "Individual Numbers" should be printed on white, and the "Team Numbers" on pink cards.

We now require an "Entry Sheet" or Book on or in which to record all entries, and one can be made by ruling as in the following reduced form:

Competitor's No.	Individual Entries, Spring Meeting, etc., 18—.				
	Name.	Match.			
		No. 1.	No. 2.	No. 4.	No. 5.
1					
2					
3					
4					
5					
6					
7					
8					
9					
10					

Several entry sheets can be made and ruled on white paper, numbered as high as the Competitors' Numbers run.

For teams the entry sheets may be ruled similar to the following reduced form on pink paper, and numbered as high as the Team Numbers run:

\multicolumn{4}{c}{Team Entries, Spring Meeting, etc., 18—.}
Team No.	Organization Represented.	Captain of Team.	Match No. 3.
1			
2			
3			
4			
5			
6			
7			
8			
9			
10			

Now, suppose everything to be so far in readiness, and the entries commencing to come in. The first entry received is from Charles Ross, of Philadelphia, who enters in matches Nos. 2 and 4, enclosing therefor $2. The Secretary enters on INDIVIDUAL ENTRANCE SHEET his name on the first line and checks on that line (√) in the columns ruled for the purpose under the matches entered for (Nos. 2 and 4). He then writes in the square blank in the upper corner of the INDIVIDUAL ENTRY BLANK the figure 1. He places that blank on file, puts the money away, and is ready for the next and following entries. Team entries are, of course, treated in the same way.

Any remarks necessary may be endorsed on the Entry Blank before filing; such, for instance, as "will call for tickets," or "mail tickets;" and if the latter (and rule as to sending postage-stamps has been complied with), copy name and address on an envelope, place the stamps on, and put it away for the present.

On *May* 11, the day after close of regular entries, the Executive Officer should come to the Secretary's office, and make his target assignments, showing *target* and *hour* at which competitor is assigned to shoot.

The method of making these assignments will be shown farther on under heading of "Executive Department." For the present, we will confine ourselves to the Secretary's work.

The Executive Officer marks upon each Entry Blank (Individual and Team in turn) the hour and target—in columns left blank for that purpose—and, either simultaneously or afterwards, the Secretary, having his score tickets sorted out and at hand, copies from the Entry Blank the competitor's *number*, *name*, *date*, and *hour* of match and *target* to which he has been assigned; and having so copied, he places the score ticket or tickets in an envelope (either for the mail or to be called for), addresses it, and encloses therein a Competitor's (or Team) Number, corresponding, of course, to the number on the score ticket. The Executive Officer should come to the Secretary's office *every day*—in the evening, if convenient—up to the day preceding the opening of the meeting, to make assignments for those making late or post entries.

By these progressive stages we have now come to the duties and workings of the

EXECUTIVE DEPARTMENT.

The Executive Officer should have prepared, by the time entries commence to be received, a blank form, ruled on card-board or stout paper, as follows:

TARGET ASSIGNMENT BLANK.

Time	1	2	3	4	5	6
9.00						
9.30						
10.00						
10.30						
11.00						
11.30						
12.00						
12.30						
1.00						
1.30						
2.00						
2.30						
3.00						
3.30						
4.00						
4.30						
5.00						
5.30						

May 15, 18—.

We have six targets on our Range, numbered from 1 to 6, as shown in the column at the left of table on preceding page. The time assignments are made upon a basis of *half-hours*, the time from 9 A.M. to 5.30 P.M. being equal to $8\frac{1}{2}$ hours, or 17 half-hours for the day. An average of one minute per shot is allowed.

Thus, if we place *four men* at a target, they can each fire 7 shots (total, 28 shots) within the half-hour, and have two minutes to spare. With *five* targets (one being used for pool-shooting), we can therefore provide for *twenty men* at once, firing 140 shots every half-hour. Thus, taking our time for the day of 15 half-hours, or 450 minutes (one hour being allowed for recess or lunch), we can have at our *five targets* equal to 300 *competitors* (28 shots at each target each half-hour) firing 2100 shots per day.

Now, by referring to our *original* entries, we find the total number of shots to be provided for on the first day as follows (see Table of Receipts):

Match.						Shots.
No. 1.	15 competitors		shoot 5 shots each			= 75
No. 2.	90	"	"	7	"	= 630
No. 3.	48	" (12 teams)	"	7	" {200 yds.{500 " }	= 672
No. 4.	75	"	"	7	"	= 525
	Total..					1902

Nineteen hundred and two shots in one day, and we have time to shoot twenty-one hundred. The surplus time covers post entries, "which must take their chances of target accommodation."

The Executive Officer now takes up the Entrance Blanks, and is careful not to unnecessarily crowd a competitor—that is to say, not to assign him for different matches that he may be entered for on consecutive half-hours, if it is avoidable—and makes the assignment as follows: He writes the Competitor's Number on his ruled sheet *opposite the target*, and *under the hour or half-hour* desired; copies this assignment on the Entrance Blank; and proceeds with the next entry, and so on, until all are assigned. He places four numbers (representing four competitors) in each ruled division — target and time — until all entries are provided for.

The following shows a reduced form of the Executive Officer's assignment for the first day all made up. The competitors' numbers may be placed, as before explained, at the *discretion of the Executive Officer;* but on the following form they are placed in rotation, commencing at the top.

May 15, 18—.

Time	Target 1	Target 2	Target 3	Target 4	Target 5	Target 6
Match No. 1, 200 Yds.						
9.00	1, 2, 3, 4	5, 6, 7, 8	9, 10, 11, 12	13, 14, 15		
Match No. 2, 200 Yards.						
9.30	1, 2, 3, 4	5, 6, 7, 8	9, 10, 11, 12	13, 14, 15, 16	17, 18, 19, 20	
10.00	21, 22, 23, 24	25, 26, 27, 28	29, 30, 31, 32	33, 34, 35, 36	37, 38, 39, 40	
10.30	41, 42, 43, 44	45, 46, 47, 48	49, 50, 51, 52	53, 54, 55, 56	57, 58, 59, 60	
11.00	61, 62, 63, 64	65, 66, 67, 68	69, 70, 71, 72	73, 74, 75, 76	77, 78, 79, 80	
11.30	81, 82, 83, 84	85, 86, 87, 88	89, 90			
12.00	Lunch.					
12.30	Lunch.					
Match No. 3, 200 Yards.						
1.00	Team 1.	Team 2.	Team 3.	Team 4.	Team 5.	
1.30	Team 6.	Team 7.	Team 8.	Team 9.	Team 10.	
2.00	Team 11.	Team 12.				
Match No. 3, 500 Yards.						
2.30	Team 1.	Team 2.	Team 3.	Team 4.	Team 5.	
3.00	Team 6.	Team 7.	Team 8.	Team 9.	Team 10.	
3.30	Team 11.	Team 12.				
Match No. 4, 500 Yards.						
4.00	1, 2, 3, 4	5, 6, 7, 8	9, 10, 11, 12	13, 14, 15, 16	17, 18, 19, 20	
4.30	21, 22, 23, 24	25, 26, 27, 28	29, 30, 31, 32	33, 34, 35, 36	37, 38, 39, 40	
5.00	41, 42, 43, 44	45, 46, 47, 48	49, 50, 51, 52	53, 54, 55, 56	57, 58, 59, 60	
5.30	61, 62, 63, 64	65, 66, 67, 68	69, 70, 71, 72	73, 74, 75		

Thus, we have assigned all original entries in one day, and provide for a maximum of entries equal to 320 individual competitors.

The match (No. 5) of the second day can be made out in the same manner on another ruled sheet; but as the number of entries will probably be much less than on the first day, and as all day may be devoted to this one match, it is unnecessary to recapitulate all the details.

A cannon, loud bell, or gong should be fired, sounded, or struck *every half-hour* throughout the day, from 9 A.M. to 5.30 P.M., thus announcing to all upon the ground the commencement and expiration of the half-hours.

THE STATISTICAL DEPARTMENT

claims our next attention. For this department (and, in fact, for all departments upon the Range) a plentiful supply of pens, ink, paper, hammers, tacks, pins, rubbers, etc., should be provided. Adjoining this department should be a secluded spot for reporters for newspapers. And here it may be remarked that politeness and civility, combined with a cheerful willingness to oblige and accommodate members of the press, is sure to be rewarded, these gentlemen being always quick to appreciate attention or resent discourtesy. Every reasonable facility (by means to be devised by the officer in charge) should be given them to obtain and copy any scores, names, or other information desired.

Upon the Statistical Officer rests the responsibility of correctly computing the scores made, and of deciding upon and announcing the winners, etc. His announcement being of course official, great care should be taken, and every precaution used, to guard against mistakes.

During the progress of the meeting, an authorized assistant gathers from the scorers the score tickets as fast as they are filled up, and hands them to the Statistical Officer, who, after having received all (which can be determined by examining the record of entries), makes up the list of Prize Winners, and bulletins it. In case of an exact tie, requiring to be shot off, he communicates with the Executive Officer, who names the target and hour for its settlement, and the Statistical Officer thereupon bulletins the fact with all particulars.

THE FINANCIAL DEPARTMENT,

superintended by the Financial Officer, has charge of all finances during the meeting. The gate-keepers are under his direction, and pool tickets are sold, and bull's-eyes afterwards redeemed, at his headquarters.

The form, manner of recording, selling, and redeeming

Pool and Bull's-eye Tickets have many varieties; and, instead of detailing any particular system, the following objective rules are given, and may be elaborated as seems best:

A pool ticket is sold for ten cents, good for *one shot* at *any pool target*, at *any distance*, during the meeting. Mr. A—— (who uses a military rifle) buys one, and goes to Target 6 at 200 yards; and upon presenting his ticket to the scorer (who marks "Military" on it), is allowed to shoot. He makes a bull's-eye, and receives a bull's-eye ticket from the scorer, marked "Bull's-eye, 200 yards. Military Rifle." In the evening he presents the same, and receives its pro-rata equivalent in money. Mr. B—— (who shoots an "any rifle," so called from being "anything but military") does the same as Mr. A—— (the scorer marking on the pool ticket he presents "Any"), and receives his bull's-eye ticket, denoting a bull's-eye made at so many yards with an "any" rifle, etc.

The scorers at pool targets are required to keep a memorandum of *how many* "any" *and how many* "military" bull's-eye tickets he gives out. This is easily recorded by giving him at the opening a certain number of each, that number, with balance returned deducted from it, gives the number issued; and the pool tickets collected by the scorers at the firing-point, and afterwards handed to the Financial Officer, show of course the number of each class ("any" or "military") from which the fifty-per-cent. division of bull's-eyes is to be made.

RANGE OFFICERS.

About one Range Officer to every five or six targets should be present at the firing-points during shooting, and should be thoroughly familiar with the shooting regulations, so as to be able promptly to decide or settle any dispute or objection.

An appeal from his decision may be taken to the Executive Officer.

In case of a disputed shot, the Range Officer should first examine the target through a telescope, and endeavor to decide in that manner the justness of the claim.

COMMITTEES.

A quorum of the *Board of Directors or Executive Committee* should be on the Range during the meeting—if not all the time, at least at a certain hour each day, in order to act promptly in case of protests, should any occur.

Should a protest be made, and an appeal taken from the decision of the Executive Officer (which is necessary to bring it before the higher authority), it is well to ascertain the hour at which such meeting will be held, and promptly notify all parties concerned to be present thereat.

The *Prize Committee* should endeavor (if practicable and safe) to have the prizes on exhibition on the Range during the meeting. They may be presented to the winners the same day, if thought advisable ; or, if they are plentiful enough and will make a good show, they may be held over, and formally presented, with appropriate addresses, music, etc., after the meeting.

A proper receipt should be taken for every prize.

The *Range Committee* should see before the meeting that targets and appurtenances are in perfect condition, and (as they are supposed to be well qualified) should individually act as Range Officers during the meeting, supervising everything, seeing that all works harmoniously and well, and using their best endeavors to secure such a result.

A source of revenue can probably be obtained by leasing the privilege of selling refreshments upon the Range, either during a meeting or for the entire season, and should be in the hands of this committee.

Other sources of income are practicable in building lockers upon the Range, and renting them to riflemen at a stated sum per year; in hiring out rifles at so much per day or hour; and in the sale of ammunition.

CONDUCT OF SIMPLE MATCHES.

Having now taken the reader through all the intricate details of a meeting (which details are applicable to any increased numbers of matches, competitors, and targets), we will next see how to conduct, by a single-entry process, as it were, a simple match with about fifty competitors. One officer can easily manage the whole business, take entries, make assignments, and run the match in manner as follows:

A record of the *names* of competitors entering must be kept in ink or pencil on a sheet of paper, piece of card-board, or convenient book, a column on the left having been previously numbered from 1 up to, say, 50.

As an entry is made, the *name* and *rifle* of the competitor should be written on a score ticket numbered to correspond with the number of his entry. All entries having been received (which need not be decided until at the firing-point, and a few minutes before the time set for the match to begin), the officer in charge sees the total number of his entries to be fifty; so, having five targets, he equalizes these fifty into squads of ten at each target, and announces aloud that "holders of tickets numbered from 1 to 10 inclusive go on target 1; numbers 11 to 20 inclusive, on target 2; numbers 21 to 30, on target 3; numbers 31 to 40, on target 4; and numbers 41 to 50, on target 5;" or he may reverse or change the order if he chooses.

It is generally easy to secure the voluntary services of five spectators as scorers; and these having been obtained, and stationed one at each target, everything is in readiness to commence the match. While it is in progress, the Executive Officer should stay at the firing-points, preserve order, prevent competitors and spectators from crowding on the score-keepers, be ready with a copy of the Regulations to settle any dispute, test triggers, see that everything is conducted fairly, and be wherever his presence is required. He should collect the tickets from the score-keepers as fast as they are filled up and signed; and when all are obtained, should compare the number of tickets with the total number of entries, verify the additions, and announce the winners.

These instructions are general, and will apply

to all small or simple matches lacking the dignity or importance of a meeting.

Some designs of score tickets suitable for such matches are shown farther on.

GENERAL INSTRUCTIONS FOR SCORE-KEEPERS.
APPLICABLE TO A "MEETING" CONDUCTED UPON PLAN EXPLAINED.

Required at Each Firing-point.—Danger-flag; camp-stool; 3 and 6 lb. trigger-testers; pencil, sharpened at both ends; and a watch, regulated before shooting commences with standard time, and used to show the half-hours, and to enforce the rule of one minute per shot.

To Commence Firing.—Lower the danger-flag, and announce "Commence firing."

To Cease Firing (which must be enforced simultaneously at all targets at *expiration of each half-hour*, or for any other cause).—Raise the danger-flag, and order "Cease firing."

Score Cards.—Deliver these *only* to the person authorized to collect them.

Scoring.—1. Verify the *color* of score ticket with *distance*. Verify the *target, hour, match,* and *rifle*. (If latter is not down, ascertain what weapon is used, and write it yourself.)

2. Test trigger of weapon of each competitor at least once during the match. *Military* rifles, 6 lbs.; *any* rifle, 3 lbs.

3. The competitor must finish his score within the *thirty minutes* succeeding the time designated on his score card, unless otherwise stated.

4. As each shot is signalled, call in a loud voice the name of competitor and value of the shot; and upon completion add up and verify total score, detach and hand competitor the coupon, and announce, in like manner, his name and the total points made.

5. *The marking as signalled cannot be questioned or debated.* All objections from competitors must be *at once* referred to a Range Officer.

6. *Hold no conversation with competitors.* Attend solely to your own business. If anything is wrong, call a Range Officer, and *let him do the talking.*

7. When a danger-signal is shown at your target (unless as a cautionary signal before marking a shot), raise your own danger-flag, order "Cease firing," and keep your flag up until target is clear. A competitor, ready to shoot at such a moment should be required to *unload his rifle*, or (if a muzzle-loading weapon) remove the cap.

8. Caution each competitor about to shoot "Target ———" (stating its number or designation).

9. If he shoots on the wrong target, *cease firing*, and report it to a Range Officer.

10. Permit no firing except as a score in a match.

11. If *two shots* are marked *consecutively* at your target when one shot only has been fired, give the competitor the one of *highest value*.

12. When a competitor *retires*, write the word "retired" after his unfinished score, and do not add up.

13. Offer no suggestions to competitors. Do no "coaching," but simply keep the score.

GENERAL INSTRUCTIONS FOR MARKERS.

These consist principally in keeping a sharp lookout all the time, seeing that an ample supply of all things necessary is at hand, and being *prompt* but *sure*, rather than too quick and careless, in marking.

In case of a *shot* (not the outside "splash" of the bullet on an iron target) *touching* the *edge* of the bull's-eye, or centre or inner lines, give the shot the benefit of the *touch* by signalling its *highest value.*

Avoid conversation, and pay strict attention to *business.*

Should two shots be made simultaneously, or nearly so, on the one target, raise the danger-signal, and mark both shots.

Note.—At Creedmoor, when a competitor fires on the wrong target (which will always explain the "two shots" spoken of above), the marker is instructed to raise his danger-signal, and keep the target idle for fifteen minutes; but the writer never could understand the object of this, as it inflicts an unjust punishment upon all other competitors at that target.

REGULATIONS
OF
THE NATIONAL RIFLE ASSOCIATION OF AMERICA.
(*Adopted* 1878.)

I.—MANAGEMENT.

A.—SPRING AND FALL MEETINGS.

1. The annual meetings for competitions will be conducted by an Executive Officer, wearing a *tri-colored* badge; aided by a Statistical Officer, wearing a *blue* badge; a Financial Officer, wearing a *white* badge; and assistants, wearing *red* badges.

2. The Executive Officer shall have control of the Range for the conduct of matches.

3. The Statistical Officer shall have charge of all statistics.

4. The Financial Officer shall have charge of all finances connected with these meetings.

B.—OTHER COMPETITIONS.

1. All other association competitions will be conducted by an

Officer or Director of the Association, or other competent person, designated by the Senior Officer or Director present on the Range at the hour of shooting, unless previously designated. In the absence of Officers and Directors, the Assistant Secretary or Superintendent of Range shall act as, or designate an, Executive Officer.

II.—GENERAL REGULATIONS.

1. During the progress of a match, no one, except the officers and employés of the Association, the competitors and the score-keepers, will be permitted within the ropes without special permission of the Executive Officer.

2. The squads of competitors will be stationed not less than four yards in rear of the firing-points, where each competitor must remain until called by the score-keeper to take his position at the firing-point, and until he has completed his score. The score-keepers will be seated close to, and in rear of, the firing-point stakes.

3. Score-keepers shall, as each shot is signalled, call in a loud voice the name of the competitor and the value of the shot, and at the conclusion of the score of each competitor, announce in like manner his name and total score.

Competitors must pay attention to the scores as announced and recorded, so that any error may be promptly investigated.

4. All competitors will be allowed to examine the records of the score-keeper during the progress of any match.

5. All protests and objections must be made to the Executive Officer in charge of the match; or, in his absence, to one of his assistants. In case a competitor is dissatisfied with the decision of the latter, he may appeal to the Executive Officer.

6. Any competitor feeling himself aggrieved by the ruling of an Executive Officer may make to the Secretary a statement of his grievance in writing, giving the names of two or more witnesses in the case, which shall be handed to the Executive Committee at its

first meeting thereafter for its consideration. The decision of the Executive Committee shall be final, subject, however, to the discretion of said Committee, or any two members of it, to refer the matter to the Board of Directors for its decision.

7. These regulations, and such directions as the Executive Officer may give, must be rigidly complied with by competitors and all other persons upon the Range grounds.

III.—RIFLES.

The rifles allowed to be used in the competitions are—1st. Military rifles; 2d. Any rifle; and must comply with the following conditions, viz.:

1. MILITARY RIFLES, weight (without bayonet) not to exceed 9 lbs. 4 oz. Stock, sufficiently strong for military purposes, and such as to admit the use of a sling; minimum pull of trigger, six pounds. Sights to be of *bona-fide* military pattern, to be attached to the barrel, and to be without any movable adjustment other than a hinged flap and sliding-bar, to be moved by hand only. In military team matches (unless otherwise specified), competitors must use the rifle with which the organization to which they belong is armed, at public expense. Filing or altering the sights of such rifles, or of the rifles used by the National Guard, or Regular forces (except as authorized by the military authorities thereof), or using them in any other way than as originally intended, is prohibited, except that the sliding-bar of the rear sight may be inverted, and lines drawn to mark the centre. Sights may be blackened, but not whitened or colored. Any pad or shoe for the heel of the butt is disallowed.

2d. ANY RIFLE, maximum weight 10 lbs., minimum pull of trigger 3 lbs., sights of any description, except telescope, magnifying, and such front aperture sights as solid disks or bushes pierced in the centre, which cover the target so as to conceal the danger-signal when displayed. No stirrup constructed of metal or other substance, connected to the rifle by straps of any kind, for the purpose of taking up or lessening its recoil, will be allowed in any of the matches of this Association.

3. Competitors shall submit their rifles and ammunition for inspection whenever required.

4. No hair or set triggers will be allowed.

5. No fixed or artificial rests will be allowed.

6. In all competitions confined to the use of breech-loaders, the gun shall be loaded at the breech with fixed ammunition.

IV.—AMMUNITION.

1. In all competitions, unless otherwise specified, any ammunition may be used, and must be provided by the competitors.

V.—TARGETS.

The targets are divided into three classes, and shall be of the following sizes:

1. *Third Class*, to be used at all distances up to, and including, 300 yards—Target, 4 × 6 feet.

    Bull's-eye, circular, 8 inches in diameter.
    Centre,   " 26 "   "
    Inner,   " 46 "   "
    Outer, remainder of target.

2. *Second Class*, to be used at all distances over 300, to, and including, 600 yards—Target, 6 × 6 feet.

    Bull's-eye, circular, 22 inches in diameter.
    Centre,   " 38 "   "
    Inner,   " 54 "   "
    Outer, remainder of target.

3. *First Class*, to be used at all distances over 600 yards—Target, 6 × 12 feet.

    Bull's-eye, circular, 36 inches in diameter.
    Centre,   " 54 "   "
    Inner, square, 6 feet × 6 feet.
    Outer, remainder of target.

VI.—MARKING, SCORING, AND SIGNALLING.

1. Bull's-eye, counts 5; signal, white circular disk.
    Centre, " 4; " red "
    Inner, " 3; " white and black "
    Outer, " 2; " black "
    Ricochet, scored R; " red flag waved twice, right and left, in front of the target. Ricochet hits will be marked out after the flag-signal.

2. When a shot strikes the angle iron upon which the target stands, the marker will open the trap and raise and lower his flag three times in front of the target.

3. Any objection to the scoring of a shot as signalled, or to one not signalled, must be made before another shot is fired.

4. Any alteration of a scoring-ticket must be witnessed by an officer in charge of the firing-point, and endorsed with his initials.

VII.—RUNNING DEER.

1. Will be run only by signal from the firing-point. Any rifle may be used, provided the sights are over the centre of the barrel. Position, standing; distance, 100 yards, unless otherwise prescribed. A fine of ten cents will be imposed for firing when out of bounds, not firing, or for hitting the haunch.

SCORING AND SIGNALLING.

    Bull's-eye, white disk, counts 4.
    Centre, red " " 3.
    Outer, black " " 2.
    Haunch, white disk, with black cross, scoring H.

VIII.—MATCHES.

1. The commencement of matches at the Spring and Fall meetings will be signalled by the firing of two guns, 15 minutes apart.

The first will be the signal for competitors and score-keepers to assemble at the firing-points, and the second to commence firing.

2. The matches will take place, if possible, in the order named in the programmes. Any deviation from the programmes will be posted upon the Bulletin Board at Headquarters as long beforehand as practicable. The posting upon such bulletin will be considered sufficient notice to all competitors of everything so posted.

3. Temporary discontinuance of matches on account of bad weather (which will be in the discretion of the Executive Officer, and applicable on all occasions), and discontinuance for noonday intermission, will be signalled by the firing of a gun. In each case the competitions will be resumed upon the firing of two guns.

4. No practice will be allowed upon the Range on any of the days of the annual meetings for competitions, unless specially authorized by the Executive Officer. This does not apply to days upon which special matches of the Association, or of affiliating associations or clubs, take place.

IX.—ENTRIES.

A.—ANNUAL MEETINGS.

1. For the State prize, and all other competitions open to military organizations, the teams shall (unless otherwise specified) consist of twelve from each regiment, battalion, company, or troop.

2. All regimental officers shall be eligible as members of such teams.

3. In all cases competitors for prizes offered to military organizations must be regularly enlisted members, in good standing, of the regiment, battalion, company, or troop which they represent, and shall have been such for at least three months prior to the match for which they are entered. All entries must be made for full teams.

4. Entries must be made at the office of the Association, in New York City, at least *one week* preceding the commencement of the

meetings. A charge of 50 per cent. additional will be imposed for all entries made after that time.

5. Competitors who are prevented from being present at any meeting shall have the entrance-fees they have paid returned after the meeting, provided that they send their tickets and give written notice to the Secretary before the day on which the prize for which they have entered has been announced for competition.

6. Competitors prevented from competing by illness will receive back their entrance-fees in full, on production of a medical certificate and their entry tickets.

7. Post entries are those made after the entry books are closed at the office of the Association.

8. The holders of the post-entry tickets may be ordered to fire whenever target accommodation can be provided; but should they be precluded from competing by deficiency of target accommodation, their entrance-fees will be returned to them, the Executive Officer not being able to guarantee accommodation for all such entries.

B.—GENERAL REGULATIONS.

1. A member of the Association entering for, or shooting in, a match on the Range must exhibit his badge.

2. A register ticket may be transferred at any time before the firing for the match has commenced by exchanging it at the office of the Statistical Officer for one having the name of the new holder. Any erasure, or the substitution of one name for another, will render the ticket invalid.

3. No post entries shall be made for any competition after the firing in such competition has commenced, unless otherwise specified.

X.—SHOOTING.

A.—ANNUAL MEETINGS.

1. Two sighting shots shall be allowed to every competitor at

each distance, on payment of ten cents a shot, unless otherwise specified.

2. Tickets for sighting shots will be sold upon the ground, and will be good for any match during the meeting. Competitors must decide, before firing, upon the number of sighting shots they will take, and hand the tickets for the same to the scorer. Sighting shots cannot be counted upon a score in any competition.

3. Competitors who, at the close of the firing on any day, have not completed the number of rounds prescribed by the conditions of a competition, shall be allowed one sighting shot when such competition is resumed, without charge.

4. In all competitions confined to military organizations, competitors shall shoot in the authorized uniform of their corps, including waist-belts.

5. In all military matches each team will be limited to an average of one minute per shot for each squad, to complete its score.

B.—GENERAL REGULATIONS.

1. In all competitions restricted to military rifles, the competitors shall place themselves at the firing-point by twos, who shall fire alternately until they have fired all their shots.

2. In other competitions, the competitors shall fire their shots alternately throughout the squad.

3. Competitors may wipe or clean out their rifles during any competition, except those restricted to the use of military rifles. In competitions of more than one distance restricted to military rifles, cleaning-out will be permitted between distances.

4. Whenever the danger-flag is displayed, competitors about to fire will be required to open the breech-block of their rifles (if breech-loaders). If they leave the firing-point, they must draw the cartridge.

5. No two competitors shall be allowed to shoot with the same rifle in the same match.

6. Any competitor delaying his squad will be passed by. In no case will the firing be delayed to enable a competitor to procure a rifle.

7. Any competitor engaged in an uncompleted match at the time fixed for the commencement of another, for which he is entered, on reporting the fact to the Executive Officer, will, if it be practicable, be assigned a target to enable him to shoot in such match upon the completion of that in which he is shooting.

XI.—POSITION.

1. In all matches (except those for cavalry carbines) the position, up to and including 300 yards, shall be standing. The left elbow may be rested against the body, provided the little finger of the left hand is in front of the trigger-guard.

2. In all military infantry matches at 400 yards, the position shall be kneeling; at distances above 400 yards any position may be taken in which the head is towards the target.

3. In cavalry-carbine matches, the position at 200 yards shall be standing; at 300 yards, kneeling; over that distance, in any position (as prescribed for infantry).

4. In all other matches at distances above 300 yards, any position may be taken without artificial rests to the rifle or body.

5. One-armed competitors shall be allowed to use false arms, without extra support, in the standing and kneeling positions, and to assume any position in the use of military rifles at distances above 400 yards, the same as is allowed for *any rifles*.

6. Sighting shots may be fired in any position, without artificial rests.

7. In all cases the gun shall be held clear of the ground.

XII.—TIES.

I.—Ties shall be decided as follows:

A.—IN INDIVIDUAL SHOOTING.

1. When the firing takes place at more than one distance, by the

score made at the longest distance; and if still a tie, and there be three distances in the competition, by the score at the second distance.*

2. By the fewest misses.
3. By the fewest outers.
4. By the fewest inners.
5. If still a tie, by inverse order of shots, counting singly from the last to the first.
6. By firing single shots at the longest range.

B.—IN TEAM SHOOTING.

1. By the aggregate scores made at the longest distance.
2. By the fewest misses.
3. By the fewest outers.
4. By the fewest inners.
5. By the competitor on each side who has made the highest score, firing five rounds at the longest distance.

II.—The names of competitors who have to shoot off ties will be posted on the Bulletin Board as soon after each match as practicable.

III.—When the ties are shot off, one sighting shot shall be allowed without charge.

IV.—Competitors not present at the firing-points at the hour named for shooting off ties lose their right to shoot.

V.—If, having forfeited their right to compete, they shall still be within the number of prize-winners, they shall take any prize that may be allotted to them by the Executive Committee.

XIII.—PRIZES.

1. Prize-winners will, upon application to the Statistical Officer

---

* Interpreted by the Board of Directors, N. R. A., to mean: Paragraph 1, by the *total number of points* made at the longest distance. Paragraphs 2, 3, and 4, by adding "in the entire score."

on the Range, receive certificates, which must be given up on receiving the prizes.

2. Prizes will be delivered on the Range at the close of the meeting, under the direction of the Executive Officer, unless otherwise specified.

3. The principal prizes at the annual Fall meeting will be formally presented to the winners at the State Arsenal, Seventh Avenue, corner Thirty-fifth Street, New York, on the Saturday following the last day of such meeting, at 8 P.M., unless otherwise announced. Winners who will be unable to attend are requested to give notice at the Headquarters Office upon the Range.

4. All prizes not claimed within one month after the match at which they have been won shall be forfeited to the Association.

XIV.—PENALTIES.

Competitors must make themselves acquainted with the Regulations, as the plea of ignorance of them will not be entertained.

DISQUALIFICATION.

Any competitor—

(*a*)—Who shall fire in a name other than his own, or who shall fire twice for the same prize, unless permitted by the conditions of the competition to do so; or,

(*b*)—Who shall be guilty of any conduct considered by the Board of Directors or the Executive Committee as discreditable; or,

(*c*)—Who shall, in National-Guard matches, use any other ammunition than that issued to him on the ground, or in any way tamper with that so issued; or,

(*d*)—Who shall be guilty of falsifying his score, or being accessory thereto; or,

(*e*)—Who shall offer a bribe of any kind to an employé—

Shall, upon the occurrence being proved to the satisfaction of the Board of Directors or the Executive Committee, forfeit all his entrance-fees, be forever disqualified from competing at any time upon the Range of the Association, and shall not be entitled to have any prize won by him at the time or meeting awarded to him.

EXCLUSION FROM FURTHER COMPETITION.

1. Any competitor who shall be detected in an evasion of the conditions prescribed for the conduct of any match shall be ruled out of such competition.

2. Any member of a squad or firing-party who shall fire a shot from any other firing-point after the hour prescribed for his squad to fire, and before he has completed his score (except in pursuance of orders), shall be disqualified in that competition.

3. Any competitor, in any meeting or match, refusing to obey any instructions of the Executive Officer or his assistants, or violating any of these regulations, or being guilty of unruly or disorderly conduct, or being intoxicated, will be immediately ruled out of all further competition during such meeting or match, and forfeit his entrance-fees; and may also be reported to the Board of Directors or the Executive Committee, and be by them disqualified from use of the Range.

4. Any competitor firing when the danger-flag or trap-disk is shown at the target or firing-point, or knowingly discharging his rifle except at a target to which he has been assigned, or into the blowing-off pits, or as may be directed by an officer, shall be debarred from all further competitions during the meeting, and shall forfeit his entrance-fees. This shall not apply to a competitor accidentally firing at the wrong target when no danger-disk is up.

5. Any person discharging a rifle or snapping a cap within the enclosure, except in accordance with the regulations for shooting, may, at the discretion of the Executive Officer, be required to leave the ground.

6. Any competitor or other person found with a loaded rifle, except at the firing-points and when about to shoot, shall be debarred from further competition during that meeting or competition.

7. Any person, whether a competitor or not, interfering with any of the firing-squads, or annoying them in any way, will be at once expelled from the ground.

8. Any competitor discharging his rifle accidentally, either by his own want of care or by reason of any defect in the rifle, shall be disqualified from further competition in the match.

9. Should a competitor lose his register-ticket, omit to take it to the firing-point, fail to attend at the prescribed hour, or give a wrong ticket, and so by his own neglect miss the opportunity given to him of competing for the prize for which his ticket was issued, his claim in regard to such competition shall be cancelled.

10. Any person firing at a wrong target will be fined $1, or be debarred from further competition; or both, in the discretion of the Executive Officer.

11. Any competitor, being a member, who shall neglect to wear conspicuously his badge of membership in any competition shall have his score disallowed.

12. Any person ruled out of any meeting or competition shall forfeit all entrance-fees.

XVI.

1. All regulations heretofore adopted, and inconsistent herewith, are hereby repealed.

2. These regulations shall take effect immediately.

NOTE BY AUTHOR.—The above Regulations govern all competitions at Creedmoor, as well as nearly all Ranges conforming to the N. R. A. targets, and will cover all points necessary. One suggestion, however, is made which will be found to materially aid quick progress of matches—viz., to establish a rule that any "competitor disputing a shot, or the marker's signal, be required to pay $1 if his claim is proved groundless." The benefit of such a rule will be demonstrated by experience.

The following, taken from the By-laws of the National Rifle Association of America, has been inserted here as being of interest to all domestic Rifle Associations or Clubs already formed, or in process of formation.

The advantages of having scores made by the various Rifle Organizations throughout the country printed in the one book (the National Rifle Association Report), where comparisons can be readily made, are so apparent to the writer, and, he believes, cannot fail to be appreciated by those interested, that any further recommendation is considered unnecessary.

EXTRACT FROM THE BY-LAWS OF THE NATIONAL RIFLE ASSOCIATION.

AFFILIATED ASSOCIATIONS AND CLUBS.

1. Any Rifle Association or Club practising in accordance with the rules of this Association may become affiliated with it upon payment of twenty-five dollars a year.

2. The members of all affiliating associations or clubs shall be entitled to all the privileges of annual members of this Association at its Spring and Fall Meetings, and to the use of the Range for one week previously. Members of affiliating associations or clubs which are organized and have their headquarters more than one hundred miles from Creedmoor, and who reside where their organizations are located, shall be entitled to the use of the Range at all times during the year for which such organization has affiliated.

3. Affiliating associations or clubs shall also be entitled:

First.—To have the names and addresses of their officers for that year, and the scores made during the year at its two principal matches, to be certified as correct by its Secretary, published in each annual report of this Association.

Second.—To receive the bronze medal of this Association for competition among its members in such manner as it shall prescribe.

Third.—To receive twenty-five copies of its Annual Report, and copies of all regulations, programmes, circulars, or other publications issued by this Association during the year, without charge.

Fourth.—To refer to the Board of Directors of this Association any question in relation to Rifle Practice for their decision.

4. Applications for affiliation must be accompanied with a check for the annual dues, a copy of the Constitution and By-laws of the affiliating society, and a roll of its officers and number of members.

Form of Score Ticket for Matches of Meeting, Page 91.

(PLATE No. 1.)

(White Ticket.)

..................Meeting, ...Rifle Association, 18.....

No. | No.

MATCH 1. 200 Yards.

Name, ...

Rifle, ... *At* ......*o'clock,*......*M.* *Target,* ....

1	2	3	4	5	Total.

Score-keeper's Signature,

....

MATCH 1.

200 Yards.

1	2	3	4	5	Total.

To be detached by Score-keeper and returned to Competitor.

FORM OF SCORE TICKET FOR MATCHES OF MEETING, PAGE 91.

(White Ticket.)

(PLATE No. 2.)

...... MEETING, ... RIFLE ASSOCIATION, 18......							No.
MATCH 2. 200 Yards.							
Name, ...							
Rifle, ... *At* .... *o'clock,* .... *M. Target,*							
1	2	3	4	5	6	7	Total.
Score-keeper's Signature, ...							

							No.
MATCH 2. 200 Yards.							
1	2	3	4	5	6	7	Total.
To be detached by Score-keeper and returned to Competitor.							

SCORE TICKET.

FORM OF SCORE TICKET FOR MATCHES OF MEETING, PAGE 93.

(PLATE No. 4.)

(Yellow Ticket.)

.... MEETING, ... RIFLE ASSOCIATION, 18...... | No. | No.

MATCH 4.
500 Yards.

Name, ...

Rifle, ... At .... o'clock .... M. Target, ...

1	2	3	4	5	6	7	Total.

Score-keeper's Signature, ...

MATCH 4.
500 Yards.

1	2	3	4	5	6	7	Total.

To be detached by Score-keeper and returned to Competitor.

SCORE TICKETS FOR MATCH No. 5 (Page 93), as below, except for 900 and 1000 yards change colors and distances: thus, change to 900 yards on *green ticket*; 1000 yards on *blue ticket*.

(PLATE No. 5.) (Pink Ticket.)

MATCH 5.

800 Yards.

No.

1	2	3	4	5
6	7	8	9	10
11	12	13	14	15

Total, _____

Return this to Competitor.

No.

Meeting, _____ Rifle Association, 18____

MATCH 5. 800 Yards.

Name, _____

Rifle, _____ At _____ o'clock. _____ M. Target, _____

1	2	3	4	5	6	7	8	9	10	11	12	13	14	15	Total.

Score-keeper's Signature, _____

SCORE TICKET.

SCORE TICKETS FOR MATCH No. 3 (Page 92), as below, except for 500 yards change color and distance: thus, change to 500 yards on *yellow ticket*.

(PLATE No. 3.)

(White Ticket.)

MEETING, ... RIFLE ASSOCIATION, 18......

MATCH 3. 200 Yards.

No. | No.

Organization, ...
Team Captain, ...
Rifle, ... At .... o'clock, ... M. Target, ...

Names.	1	2	3	4	5	6	7	Total
1								
2								
3								
4								

Aggregate, ...

Score-keeper's Signature, ...

MATCH 3. 200 Yards.

	1	2	3	4	5	6	7	Total
1								
2								
3								
4								

Aggregate, ...

To be detached by Score-keeper and returned to Captain.

A simple SCORE CARD that can be used for any match at one or two distances, five or seven shots.

No.										Competition.
Name,						Date,		18		
							Rifle,			Target,

Yards.	1	2	3	4	5	6	7	Total.	Aggregate.	Remarks.

Register-keeper's Signature,

SCORE TICKET.

A Score Ticket, with Coupon, to be detached and returned to the competitor; good for any match at three or less distances, with ten or less shots at each distance.

No. ....

.... Competition at .... 18.........

Name, ...

Rifle, ... Target, ...

Yards.	1	2	3	4	5	6	7	8	9	10	Total.	Aggregate.

Register-keeper's Signature, ...

No. ....

....
Date, ...

Name, ...

	1	2	3	4	5	6	7	8	9	10	Total.

Aggregate, ============

The following is a simple form of SCORE TICKET which can be used for any match at three or less distances, with any number of shots (within fifteen) at each distance.

No. ....

.... Competition.

Date, ... 18........

Name, ... Rifle, ... Target, ...

Yards.	1	2	3	4	5	6	7	8	9	10	11	12	13	14	15	Total.	Aggregate.

Register-keeper's Signature, ...

SCORE TICKET.

A simple Ticket for TEAM MATCH at any one or more distances, with ten or less shots at each distance, teams to consist of seven or less men.

Team No. ....

Yards, ...

Team representing .... Match. Date, ... 18......

Rifles. ....

No.	Name.	1	2	3	4	5	6	7	8	9	10	Total.	Team Aggregate,
1													
2													
3													
4													
5													
6													
7													

Register-keeper's Signature, ... Target, ...

A COMBINATION SCORE TICKET that may be used in Individual Matches at any distance or distances up to 1000 yards, and any number of shots within thirty. Color for *distance*, or the *same ticket*, or a *separate ticket* from same lot, may be used at will.

No.	Competition for _____ 18___.
	Name, _____ At _____ Range.
	Hour, _____ o'clock, ____ M. At Target _____

Yards.	No. of Shots.	Rifle.	10 Shots.		10 Shots.		10 Shots.		Total.
			5 Shots.	5 Shots.	5 Shots.	5 Shots.	5 Shots.	5 Shots.	
100									
200									
300									
400									
500									
600									
700									
800									
900									
1000									

Scorer's Signature, _____ Aggregate, _____

Address, _____

RIFLE CLUBS AND ASSOCIATIONS IN THE UNITED STATES.

The following list has been carefully compiled in alphabetical order, and, though some omissions have unavoidably been made, owing to lack of information, it is believed to be as complete, up to time of publication (1879), as possible.

Akron Rifle Association, Akron, Ohio.
Albion Rifle Club, Albion, N. Y.
Amateur Long-Range Rifle Club, San Francisco, Cal.
Amateur Rifle Club, Atlanta, Idaho Ter.
Amateur Rifle Club, Attleboro', Mass.
Amateur Rifle Club, Augusta, Ga.
Amateur Rifle Club, East Saginaw, Mich.
Amateur Rifle Club, New Britain, Conn.
Amateur Rifle Club, New York City, N. Y.
Amateur Rifle Club, Salt Lake City, Utah.
Amateur Rifle Club, Stamford, Conn.
Amateur Rifle Club, Syracuse, N. Y.
American Off-hand Rifle Association, New York City, N. Y.
American Off-hand Rifle Club, Union Hill, N. J.
American Rifle Association, Mount Vernon, N. Y.
American-Union Rifle Association, Meriden, Conn.
Androscoggin Rifle Club, Lewiston, Me.
Atlantic Rifle Club, Milwaukee, Wis.
Augusta Rifle Association, Augusta, Ga.
Ausable Valley Rifle Club, Keeseville, N. Y.
Ballard Rifle Club, New York City, N. Y.
Bath Rifle Club, Bath, N. Y.
Bay View Rifle Association, Buffalo, N. Y.
Bergen Point Rifle Club, Bergen Point, N. J.
Berkshire Sportman's Club, Pittsfield, Mass.
Berlin Rifle Club, Berlin, Conn.

Bloomington Rifle Association, Bloomington, Ill.
Blydenburgh Rifle Club, Syracuse, N. Y.
Boone Rifle Club, Boone, Iowa.
Bridgeport Rifle Association, Bridgeport, Conn.
Brocton Rifle Club, Gardner, Mass.
Boston Highlands Rifle Club, Boston, Mass.
Boston Rifle Club, Boston, Mass.
Brooklyn Rifle Club, Brooklyn, N. Y.
Brooklyn Schützencorps, Brooklyn, N. Y.
Burlington Rifle Club, Burlington, Vt.
California Rifle Association, San Francisco, Cal.
California Schützencorps, San Francisco, Cal.
Capital City Rifle Association, Des Moines, Iowa.
Carlisle Rifle Association, Carlisle, Pa.
Centennial Rifle Club, Jersey City Heights, N. J.
Central Railroad Rifle Club, Jersey City, N. J.
Chicago Rifle Club, Chicago, Ill.
Cincinnati Amateur Rifle Club, Cincinnati, Ohio.
Cincinnati Sporting Club, Cincinnati, Ohio.
Citizen's Rifle Club, Wallingford, Conn.
Columbia Rifle Association of D. C., Washington, D. C.
Columbia Rifle Association, Guttenburgh, N. J.
Columbia Rifle Association, West End, N. J.
Columbus Rifle Club, Columbus, Ohio.
Connecticut Rifle Association, Hartford, Conn.
Connecticut Rifle Association, Stamford, Conn.
Continental Rifle Club, New Orleans, La.
Creedmoor Rifle Club, Creedmoor, L. I.
Crescent City Rifle Club, New Orleans, La.
Dayton Schützenverein, Dayton, Ohio.
Dearborn Rifle Club, Chicago, Ill.
Deseret Rifle Club, Salt Lake City, Utah.
Detroit Schützenverein, Detroit, Mich.

East Coventry Rifle Club, East Coventry, Pa.
Eastern Sharpshooters' Association, Baltimore, Md.
Easton Rifle Association, Easton, Pa.
East Saginaw Amateur Rifle Club, East Saginaw, Mich.
Elgin Amateur Rifle Club, Elgin, Ill.
Elizabeth Rifle Club, Elizabeth, N. J.
Emmet Guard Rifle Club, Virginia City, Nev.
Empire Rifle Club, New York City, N. Y.
Empire State Rifle Association, Syracuse, N. Y.
Empire State Rifle Club, Watertown, N. Y.
Ethan Allen Rifle Association, Vergennes, Vt.
Flushing Rifle Association, Flushing, L. I., N. Y.
Forest and Stream Rifle Club, Boston, Mass.
Forest City Rifle Association, Euclid, Ohio.
Fort Wayne Rifle Association, Fort Wayne, Ind.
Franklin Rifle Club, Hartford, Conn.
Fulton Rifle Association, Stockton, Pa.
Galveston Rifle Club, Galveston, Texas.
Gardner Rifle Club, Gardner, Mass.
Garnerville Rifle Club, Garnerville, N. Y.
G. A. Thomas Post (G. A. R.) Rifle Club, Chicago, Ill.
Geneva Rifle Club, Geneva, N. Y.
German Fusileer Rifle Club, Charleston, S. C.
German Hussars' Rifle Club, Charleston, S. C.
German Rifle Club, New York City, N. Y.
German Shooting Club, Savannah, Ga.
German Union Rifle Club, Meriden, Conn.
Girard Rifle Club, Philadelphia, Pa.
Glen Alger Rifle Association, Harrisville, Mich.
Golden Colorado Rifle Club, Beaver Brook, Col.
Green Bay and Fort Howard Sharpshooters' Union, Green Bay, Wis.
Greenville Rifle Association, Greenville, Mich.

Hackensack Rifle Association, Hackensack, N. J.
Harrisville Rifle Association, Harrisville, Mich.
Hartford Rifle Club, Hartford, Conn.
Harvard College Rifle Club, Cambridge, Mass.
Havre de Grace Rifle Association, Havre de Grace, Md.
Helena Rifle Club, Helena, Ark.
Helena Rifle Club, Helena, Montana Ter.
Hellwig Rifle Club, New York City, N. Y.
Helvetia Rifle Club, New York City, N. Y.
Holyoke Rifle Club, Holyoke, Mass.
Houston Rifle Club, Houston, Texas.
Hudson River Rifle Association, Poughkeepsie, N. Y.
Huntsville Rifle Club, Huntsville, Ala.
Independent Rifle Club, New Haven, Conn.
Industrial Rifle Club, Jersey City, N. J.
Institute of Technology Rifle Club, Boston, Mass.
Irish-American Rifle Club, Boston, Mass.
Irish-American Rifle Club, New York City, N. Y.
Irish-American Rifle Club, Greenwich, Conn.
Irish Rifle Club, Cincinnati, Ohio.
Ithaca Rifle Club, Ithaca, N. Y.
Jackson Rifle Club, Jackson, Mich.
Jamaica Rod and Rifle Association, Jamaica, L. I., N. Y.
Jersey Schützencorps, Jersey City, N. J.
Keystone Rifle Club, Philadelphia, Pa.
Lake View Rifle Club, Chicago, Ill.
Lawrence Rifle Club, Lawrence, Mass.
Leather-Stocking Rifle Club, Goshen, N. Y.
Leicester Rifle Club, Leicester, Mass.
Long-Range Rifle Club, Louisville, Ky.
Louisiana Field and Artillery Rifle Club, New Orleans, La.
Macon Rifle Association, Macon, Ga.
Maine Rifle Club, Portland, Me.

Malone Rifle Club, Malone, N. Y.
Man Island Rifle Club, Man Island, Cal.
Marinette Rifle Club, Marinette, Wis.
Marion Rifle Club, Jersey City, N. J.
Maryland Rifle Club, Baltimore, Md.
Massachusetts Rifle Association, Boston, Mass.
Maynard Rifle Club, Wheeling, West Va.
McClellan Rifle Club, Philipsburgh, N. J.
Medford Amateur Rifle Association, Medford, Mass.
Middlebury Rifle Club, Middlebury, Vt.
Middletown Rifle Association, Middletown, Conn.
Milwaukee Rifle Club, Milwaukee, Wis.
Mohawk Valley Rifle Association, Utica, N. Y.
Morrison Rifle Club, Morrison, Ill.
Mount Mansfield Rifle Club, Stowe, Vt.
Mount Washington Rifle Club, Haverhill, Mass.
Munroe Rifle Club, Munroe, Mich.
National Rifle Association of America.
National Rifle Club, South Vernon, Vt.
Newark Amateur Rifle Club, Newark, N. J.
Newark Rifle Club, Wayne Co., N. Y.
Newark Schützen Society, Newark, N. J.
New Britain Rifle Club, New Britain, Conn.
Newburgh Rifle Association, Newburgh, N. Y.
New Haven Rifle Association, New Haven, Conn.
New Jersey Rifle and Gun Club, Ridgewood, N. J.
New Jersey Schützencorps, Newark, N. J.
New Jersey State Rifle Association, Elizabeth, N. J.
New Orleans Rifle Club, New Orleans, La.
Newtown Rifle Club, Newtown, L. I., N. Y.
New York Rifle Club, New York City, N. Y.
New York City Schützencorps, New York City, N. Y.
New York Schützencorps, New York City, N. Y.

New York Stock Exchange Rifle Club, New York City, N. Y.
Norristown Rifle Club, Norristown, Pa.
North Vallejo Rifle Club, North Vallejo, Cal.
Northwestern Rifle Association, Milwaukee, Wis.
Norwich Rifle Club, Norwich, Conn.
Oakland Amateur Rifle Club, Oakland, Cal.
Ogdensburgh Rifle Club, Ogdensburgh, N. Y.
Old Dominion Rifle Association, Richmond, Va.
Omaha Rifle Club, Omaha, Neb.
Owl's Head Rifle Club, Bay Ridge, L. I., N. Y.
Parthian Rifle Club, Hudson, N. Y.
Peck's Rifle Club, Chicago, Ill.
Pennsylvania Rifle Club, Philadelphia, Pa.
Petaluma Rifle Club, Petaluma, Cal.
Pioneer Rifle Club, Plainfield, N. J.
Pioneer Rifle Club, Salt Lake City, Utah.
Plainfield Rifle Association, Plainfield, N. J.
Plattsburgh Rifle Association, Plattsburgh, N. Y.
Port Henry Rifle Association, Port Henry, N. Y.
Post 28 G. A. R. Rifle Club, Chicago, Ill.
Potsdam Rifle Association, Potsdam, N. Y.
Practice Rifle Club, Shakopee, Minn.
Prospect Hill Rifle Club, Yorkville, N. Y.
Putnam Rifle and Sporting Club, Putnam, Conn.
Queens Sportman's Club, Queens, L. I., N. Y.
Rahway Rifle Club, Rahway, N. J.
Remington Rifle Association, Carlisle, Pa.
Remington Rifle Club, Oswego, N. Y.
Rhinebeck Rifle Club, Rhinebeck, N. Y.
Rhode Island Amateur Rifle Association, Providence, R. I.
Rhode Island Amateur Rifle Club, Valley Falls, R. I.
Richmond Rifle Club, Augusta, Ga.
Ridgewood Sporting Club, Ridgewood, N. J.

RIFLE CLUBS IN THE UNITED STATES.

Riverside Rifle Club, Pittsfield, Mass.
Riverton Rifle Club, Philadelphia, Pa.
Rochester Amateur Rifle Club, Rochester, N. Y.
Rochester Rifle Club, Rochester, Minn.
Rod and Gun Rifle Club, Springfield, Mass.
Rosedale Rifle Club, Rosedale, Kan.
Rossmore Rifle Club, Staten Island, N. Y.
Rutland Rifle Club, Rutland, Vt.
Sacramento Rifle Club, Sacramento, Cal.
Salem Rifle Association, Peabody, Mass.
San Rafael Rifle Club, San Rafael, Cal.
Santa Rosa Sportsman's Club, Santa Rosa, Cal.
Saratoga Rifle Club, Saratoga Springs, N. Y.
Saugatuck Rifle Club, Saugatuck, Conn.
Savannah Rifle Association, Savannah, Ga.
Savannah Schützenfest-Gesellschaft, Savannah, Ga.
Schützenpark Association, Union Hill, N. J.
Scottish-American Rifle Club, New York City, N. Y.
Selkirk Rifle Club, South Cayuga, N. Y.
Seppenfeldt Rifle Club, New York City, N. Y.
Sharpshooters' Union of the United States, Philadelphia, Pa.
Shrewsbury Rifle Club, Worcester, Mass.
Singer Rifle Club, Elizabethport, N. J.
Social Gun and Rifle Club, Philadelphia, Pa.
Sonora Rifle Club, Sonora, Cal.
South Cayuga Rifle Club, South Cayuga, N. Y.
South Orange Amateur Rifle Association, South Orange, N. J.
South Vallejo Rifle Club, South Vallejo, Cal.
Sportsman's Club, Taunton, Mass.
Springfield Amateur Rifle Club, Springfield, Mass.
St. George and St. Andrew Rifle Club, Wilmington, N. C.
State German Rifle Association, New Haven, Conn.
Staten Island Schützencorps, Staten Island, N. Y.

Syracuse Amateur Rifle Association, Syracuse, N. Y.
Syracuse Rifle Association, Syracuse, N. Y.
Tobacco City Rifle Club, Lynchburgh, Va.
Tritoner Rifle Club, New York City, N. Y.
Trojan Rifle Club, Troy, N. Y.
Tuckee Rifle Club, Tuckee, Nevada Co., Cal.
University of California Rifle Club, Berkeley, Cal.
Utah Rifle Association, Salt Lake City, Utah.
Utica Citizens' Rifle Club, Utica, N. Y.
Vicksburg Rifle Club, Vicksburg, Miss.
Vicksburg Schützenverein, Vicksburg, Miss.
Walpole Rifle Association, Walpole, Mass.
Warren Rifle Club, Warren, Ill.
Waterbury Rifle Club, Waterbury, Conn.
Watertown Rifle Club, Watertown, N. Y.
Waverly Rifle Association, Waverly, N. Y.
Waverly Rifle Club, Sayne, Pa.
West Philadelphia Rifle Club, Philadelphia, Pa.
Wheeling Rifle Club, Wheeling, West Va.
Whitneyville Amateur Rifle Club, New Haven, Conn.
Wilmington Rifle Club, Wilmington, N. C.
Woodstock Shooting Club, Woodstock, Vt.
Worcester Sportsman's Club, Worcester, Mass.
Yonkers Rifle Association, Yonkers, N. Y.
Zettler Rifle Club, New York City, N. Y.

FOREIGN RIFLE CLUBS AND ASSOCIATIONS.

This list has been much more difficult to compile than that of Domestic Clubs, several Rifle Organizations being known to exist in France, Germany, Switzerland, Belgium, etc., whose headquarters are unknown to the writer. Those given below may be received without any doubt of their authenticity.

American Rifle Club, Lima, Peru.
Auckland Rifle Association, Auckland, New Zealand.
British Columbia Rifle Association, Victoria, British Columbia, North America.
Calcutta Volunteer Rifle Association, Calcutta, India.
Cape of Good Hope Rifle Association, Cape Town, South Africa.
Cobourg Rifle Association, Cobourg, Canada.
Deccan Rifle Association, Chudderghaut, Hyderabad, India.
Demerara Rifle Association, Demerara, West Indies.
Dominion of Canada Rifle Association, Ottawa, Canada.
Eastern Province of South Africa Rifle Association, Graham Town, South Africa.
Guelph Rifle Association, Guelph, Ontario, Canada.
Hong-Kong Rifle Association, Hong-Kong, China.
Hyderabad Rifle Association, Secunderabad, India.
Irish Rifle Association, Dublin, Ireland.
Kaffrarian Rifle Association, Williams Town, South Africa.
Kimberley Rifle Association, Kimberley, South Africa.
Mauritius Rifle Association, Port Louis, Mauritius.
Metropolitan Rifle Association, Ottawa, Canada.
Miniature Rifle Club, Dublin, Ireland.
Montreal Rifle Association, Montreal, Canada.
Natal Coast Rifle Association, Port Natal, South Africa.
Natal Rifle Association, Petermaritzburg, South Africa.

National Rifle Association, London, England.
National Rifle Club, Edinburgh, Scotland.
New Brunswick Rifle Association, New Brunswick, Canada.
New South Wales Rifle Association, Sydney, Australia.
New Zealand Rifle Association, Wellington, New Zealand.
Northern India Rifle Association, Simba, India.
Ontario Rifle Association, Toronto, Canada.
Otago Rifle Association, Derudin, New Zealand.
Poona Rifle Association, Poona, India.
Port Elizabeth Rifle Association, Port Elizabeth, South Africa.
Prince Edward's Island Rifle Association, Charlottetown, Prince Edward's Island.
Province of Quebec Rifle Association, Montreal, Canada.
Provincial Rifle Association, Halifax, Nova Scotia.
Seventh Military District Rifle Association, Hamilton, Canada.
Shanghai Rifle Association, Shanghai, China.
Société Havraise de Tir, Havre, France.
South Australian Rifle Association, Adelaide, Australia.
Southern India Rifle Association, Bangalore, India.
Taranaki Rifle Association, New Plymouth, New Zealand.
Thames Rifle Association, Thames Gold Fields, New Zealand.
Ulster Rifle Association, Belfast, Ireland.
Victoria Rifle Association, Melbourne, Australia.
Victorian Rifle Association, Montreal, Canada.
Wanganui Rifle Association, Wanganui, New Zealand.
West of Scotland Rifle Association, Glasgow, Scotland.
Yokohama Rifle Association, Yokohama, Japan.

RIFLE RECORD

OF TEAM AND INDIVIDUAL MATCHES AND SCORES IN EUROPE AND AMERICA.

INTERNATIONAL LONG-RANGE MATCHES.

1874.

IRELAND versus AMERICA.

Shot at Creedmoor, September 16, 1874.

(The first International Rifle Team Contest ever shot in America.)

Between teams of six men each representing Ireland and America. Distances, 800, 900, and 1000 yards. Fifteen shots at each distance. Irish Team used Rigby rifles. American Team all shot with American breech-loaders.

Shot at the old square bull's-eye targets.

Highest possible Team total, 1080 points.

Captain of the American Team, Colonel George W. Wingate.

Captain of the Irish Team, Major Arthur B. Leech.

American Team:	Irish Team:
934 points.	931 points.

American Majority, 3 points.

1875.

IRELAND versus AMERICA.

Shot at Dollymount, Ireland, June 29, 1875.

Return match between teams of six men each representing Ireland and America. Distances, 800, 900, and 1000 yards. Fifteen shots at each distance. Irish Team used Rigby rifles. The American Team all shot with American breech-loaders.

Shot at the old square bull's-eye targets.
Highest possible Team total, 1080 points.
Captain of American Team, Colonel Henry A. Gildersleeve.
Captain of Irish Team, Major Arthur B. Leech.

AMERICAN TEAM:	IRISH TEAM:
968 points.	929 points.

American Majority, 39 points.

CANADA versus THE UNITED STATES.

SHOT AT CREEDMOOR, SEPTEMBER 25, 1875,

under the auspices of the Amateur Rifle Club of New York City.

Teams of eight men each. Distances, 800, 900, and 1000 yards. Fifteen shots at each distance.

Captain of American Team, Major-General T. S. Dakin.
Captain of Canadian Team, Captain C. R. Murray.

AMERICAN TEAM:	CANADIAN TEAM:
1409 points.	1384 points.

American Majority, 25 points.

1876.

THE FIRST INTERNATIONAL LONG-RANGE MATCH
FOR THE
AMERICAN CENTENNIAL TROPHY "PALMA"
AND THE
CHAMPIONSHIP OF THE WORLD.

First competition was shot at Creedmoor, Wednesday and Thursday, September 13 and 14, 1876.

Between teams of eight men, each representing Scotland, Ireland, Australia, Canada, and America. Distances, 800, 900, and 1000 yards. Fifteen shots at each distance upon each day.

The American Centennial Trophy "Palma."

Highest possible team score each day, 1800 points, both days = 3600 points.

Captain of American Team, Major Henry Fulton.
Captain of Irish Team, Major Arthur B. Leech.
Captain of Scotch Team, Lieut.-Col. J. H. A. Macdonald.
Captain of Australian Team, Captain A. Blannin.
Captain of Canadian Team, Major J. E. O'Reilly.

	AMERICAN TEAM:	IRISH TEAM:	SCOTCH TEAM:
First day,	1577 points.	1582 points.	1586 points.
Second day,	1549 "	1522 "	1477 "
Total,	3126 "	3104 "	3063 "

	AUSTRALIAN TEAM:	CANADIAN TEAM:
First day,	1545 points.	1490 points.
Second day,	1517 "	1433 "
Total,	3062 "	2923 "

American Majority over Ireland, 22 points.
" " " Scotland, 63 "
" " " Australia, 64 "
" " " Canada, 203 "

IRELAND versus AMERICA.

SHOT AT CREEDMOOR, SEPTEMBER 21, 1876,

under the auspices of the Amateur Rifle Club of New York City.

Teams of six men each. Distances, 800, 900, and 1000 yards. Fifteen shots at each distance.

AMERICAN TEAM:	IRISH TEAM:
1165 points.	1154 points.

American Majority, 11 points.

1877.

THE SECOND INTERNATIONAL LONG-RANGE MATCH
FOR THE
AMERICAN CENTENNIAL TROPHY "PALMA"
AND THE
CHAMPIONSHIP OF THE WORLD.

Second competition shot at Creedmoor on Thursday and Friday, September 13 and 14, 1877, between teams of eight men each, representing Great Britain and Ireland and America. Conditions same as first competition in 1876.

Captain of American Team, Major-General Thomas S. Dakin.
Captain of British Team, Sir Henry J. Halford, Bart.

American Team:	British Team:
First day, 1655 points.	1629 points.
Second day, 1679 "	1613 "
Total, 3334 "	3242 "

American Majority, 92 points.

CANADA versus THE UNITED STATES.

Shot at Toronto, Canada, September 3, 1877.

Teams of six men each, representing respectively the Amateur Rifle Club of New York City and the Victoria Rifle Club of Hamilton, Ontario, Canada. Distances, 800, 900, and 1000 yards. Fifteen shots at each distance.

Captain of American Team, Lieut.-Col. E. Harrison Sanford.
Captain of Canadian Team, Lieut.-Col. J. M. Gibson.

American Team:	Canadian Team:
1083 points.	1061 points.

American Majority, 22 points.

1878.

THE THIRD INTERNATIONAL LONG-RANGE MATCH
FOR THE
AMERICAN CENTENNIAL TROPHY "PALMA"
AND THE
CHAMPIONSHIP OF THE WORLD.

Third competition shot at Creedmoor, Wednesday and Thursday, September 25 and 26, 1878.

Captain of Team, Captain William H. Jackson.

AMERICAN TEAM.
(No other Competitors.)

First day, 1660 points.
Second day, 1576 "
Aggregate, 3236 " with 17 shots to fire.

THE FIRST INTERNATIONAL MILITARY MATCH.

For a trophy presented by Honorable Henry Hilton, of New York, valued at $3000. Shot at Creedmoor during the Fall Meeting of the N. R. A., September, 1878.

Open to teams of twelve men from each of the three Military Divisions of the United States Army. One team from the United States Navy. One team representing the National Guard, or Uniformed Militia, from each State and Territory in the United States. One team each from the Regular Army, the Militia, the Volunteers and the Navy of all Countries, Provinces of Great Britain, and Provinces of Canada.

At the above competition teams entered representing respectively the Military Divisions of the Atlantic, Missouri, and Pacific,

INTERNATIONAL MILITARY PRIZE.

The "Hilton Trophy," International Military Prize.

United States Army (the latter arriving too late to compete), and the States of Connecticut, New Jersey, and New York.

Distances, 200, 500, and 600 yards. Seven shots at each distance each man. Weapon, any military rifle that has been adopted as an official arm by any State or Government.

	Scores.			
	200 yds.	500 yds.	600 yds.	Aggt.
State of New York	345	370	329	1044
State of Connecticut	345	331	227	903
Mil. Div. of the Atlantic, U. S. A.	312	311	239	862
State of New Jersey	328	301	232	861
Mil. Div. of the Missouri, U. S. A.	303	276	224	803

INTER-STATE MILITARY MATCHES.

Prize.—A Bronze Trophy, "The Soldier of Marathon."

Open to teams of twelve men each, representing the National Guard and Uniformed Militia of any State and Territory in the United States.

1875.

First Match shot at Creedmoor, October 1, 1875.

200 and 400 yards. Ten shots at each distance.

	200 yds.	400 yds.	Aggt.
State of New York, score	446	418	864
State of Connecticut, "	375	308	683

1876.

Shot at Creedmoor, September 20, 1876.

200 and 500 yards. Other conditions same as first match.

	200 yds.	500 yds.	Aggt.
State of Connecticut, score	443	386	829
State of New York, "	434	382	816

"The Soldier of Marathon," First Prize in Inter-State Military Match.

1877.

SHOT AT CREEDMOOR, SEPTEMBER 12, 1877.
Conditions as in 1876.

	200 yds.	500 yds.	Aggt.
State of California, score	499	496	995
State of Connecticut, "	505	466	971
State of New York, "	480	487	967
State of New Jersey, "	411	333	744

1878.

SHOT AT CREEDMOOR, SEPTEMBER 19, 1878.
Conditions as in 1877.

	200 yds.	500 yds.	Aggt.
State of New York, score	483	491	974
State of Connecticut, "	476	430	906
State of New Jersey, "	455	409	864
State of Rhode Island, "	461	392	853
State of Massachusetts, "	387	335	722

INTER-STATE LONG-RANGE MATCHES.

FOR A TROPHY TO BE SHOT FOR ANNUALLY.

Teams of four from all Rifle Clubs and Associations in any State or Territory of the United States that have affiliated with the National Rifle Association previous to the match. Distances, 800, 900, and 1000 yards. Fifteen shots at each distance. Any rifle.

1877.

Amateur Rifle Club of N. Y.	825	points.
Massachusetts Rifle Association	786	"
Parthian Rifle Club of N. Y.	780	"
Crescent City Rifle Club of La.	754	"
Hackensack Rifle Association of N. J.	752	"
Columbia Rifle Association of D. C.	736	"

1878.

(Conditions as above.)

Massachusetts Rifle Association	845 points.	
Amateur Rifle Club of N. Y.	836	"
Columbia Rifle Association of D. C.	737	"

INDIVIDUAL LONG-RANGE MATCHES.

INDIVIDUAL LONG-RANGE CHAMPIONSHIP OF THE UNITED STATES.

First Match for the "LEECH CUP" and Championship Gold Badge. Open to all native-born citizens of the United States, and all resident members of the Amateur Rifle Club of New York, regardless of nationality. Distances, 800, 900, and 1000 yards. Fifteen shots at each distance. Any rifle.

1875.—Won by Colonel John Bodine.

	800 yds.	900 yds.	1000 yds.	Aggt.
Score	65	69	71	205

1876.—Won by Colonel H. A. Gildersleeve.

	800 yds.	900 yds.	1000 yds.	Aggt.
Score	68	71	75	214

1877.—Won by Major H. S. Jewell.

	800 yds.	900 yds.	1000 yds.	Aggt.
Score	71	69	73	213

1878.—Won by Frank Hyde.

	800 yds.	900 yds.	1000 yds.	Aggt.
Score	69	67	69	205

COMPETITIONS FOR THE "WIMBLEDON CUP."

Shot for annually during the Fall Meeting of the N. R. A. Open to all citizens and residents of the United States. Distance, 1000 yards. Thirty shots. Any rifle.

1875 (at Wimbledon). Won by Major Henry Fulton; score, 133.
1876 (at Creedmoor). Won by Isaac L. Allen; score, 139.
1877 (at Creedmoor). Won by Dudley Selph; score, 137.
1878 (at Creedmoor). Won by Frank Hyde; score, 143.

CHAMPION'S MATCH.

Open to all comers. Any rifle. Distances, 200, 600, and 1000 yards. Ten shots at each distance.

Grand N. R. A. Gold Medal, first prize.
Grand N. R. A. Silver Medal, second prize.
Grand N. R. A. Bronze Medal, third prize.

		200 yds.	600 yds.	1000 yds.	Aggt.
1875.—1st prize.	Major Henry Fulton, score..	42	42	47	131
2d "	James Mason (of Canadian Team). " ..	37	46	43	126
3d "	Capt. R. C. Coleman, " ..	45	47	31	123
1876.—1st prize.	Lieutenant-Colonel E. H. Sanford, score..	42	47	44	133
2d "	Peter Rae (of Scotch Team), " ..	42	41	46	129
3d "	J. K. Millner (of Irish Team), " ..	37	49	43	129

			200 yds.	600 yds.	1000 yds.	Aggt.
1877.—1st prize.	Major Henry Fulton, score.	47	49	43	139
	2d "	I. L. Allen, " ..	44	49	42	135
	3d "	General T. S. Dakin, " ..	42	48	44	134
1878.—1st prize.	W. Milton Farrow, score..	46	47	46	139
	2d "	I. L. Allen, " ..	42	45	49	136
	3d "	Colonel H. F. Clark, " ..	40	50	45	135

MATCH FOR THE MILITARY CHAMPIONSHIP OF THE UNITED STATES.

First Stage.

Open to members of the Army and Navy of the United States or National Guard of any State. Distances, 200, 500, and 600 yards. Seven shots at each distance. Weapon, the military arm used by the organization of which competitor is a member.

Winner of First Prize in First Stage.

	200 yds.	500 yds.	600 yds.	Aggt.
Pvt. C. H. Eagle, 7th Regt. N. G. S. N. Y., score..	29	29	29	87

Second Stage.

Open to highest sixty in the first stage. Distances, 800, 900, and 1000 yards. Seven shots at each distance. Special military rifles. First prize, the "Gold Champion's Medal," and the "Military Championship of the United States" for one year.

Winner.

Captain J. S. Barton, 48th Regt. N. G. S. N. Y.

(Score in First Stage.)				(Score in Second Stage.)			
200 yds.	500 yds.	600 yds.	Aggt.	800 yds.	900 yds.	1000 yds.	Aggt.
30	20	30	80	31	28	18	77

The "Military Championship of the United States" Gold Medal.

SHORT-RANGE MATCHES.

"JUDD" MATCHES

of Fall Meetings of the N. R. A. at Creedmoor. Distance, 200 yards. Five shots. Any military rifle.

Winners of First Prizes.

1873.—W. Robertson, score............ 16 points (old target).
1874.—Capt. H. B. Smith, " (seven shots) 23 " "
1875.—J. Mason, " " 30 "
1876.—F. J. Fulgraff, " " 34 "
1877.—E. W. Whitlock, " " 33 "
1878.—B. McSoley, " " 33 "

"SHORT-RANGE" MATCHES

of Fall Meetings of the N. R. A. at Creedmoor. Distance, 200 yards. Five shots. Any rifle.

Winners of First Prizes.

1873.—O. Schneeloch, score............ 16 points (old target).
1874.—Joseph Turner, " (seven shots) 27 " "
1875.—Thos. R. Murphy, " " 32 "
1876.—H. F. Clark, " " 30 "
1877.—Edward Squier, " " 33 "
1878.—D. C. Millis, " " 32 "

SHORT-RANGE TEAM MATCH OF 1877.

Shot at Creedmoor during Fall Meeting of that year. Teams of five men, from Rifle Clubs and Military Organizations. Any rifle or carbine. Distances, 200 and 300 yards. Seven shots each distance.

There were twenty teams in this match, the scores made being as follows:

	200 yds.	300 yds.	Aggt.
1st Team, score	145	127	272
2d " "	143	123	266
3d " "	140	123	263
4th " "	144	119	263
5th " "	133	127	260
6th " "	138	120	258
7th " "	141	115	256
8th " "	140	114	254
9th " "	127	126	253
10th " "	136	112	248
11th " "	128	119	247
12th " "	135	107	242
13th " "	121	120	241
14th " "	128	113	241
15th " "	130	108	238
16th " "	128	105	233
17th " "	129	101	230
18th " "	126	99	225
19th " "	122	100	222
20th " "	117	76	193

SHORT-RANGE TEAM MATCH OF 1878.

Shot at Creedmoor during Fall Meeting of that year. Teams of *four* from Rifle Clubs and Military Organizations. Distances, 200 and 300 yards. Seven shots at each distance. Any rifle or carbine.

There were sixteen teams in this match, the scores made being as follows:

	200 yds.	300 yds.	Aggt.
1st Team, score	119	108	227
2d " "	116	108	224
3d " "	119	105	224
4th " "	118	102	220
5th " "	113	104	217
6th " "	110	106	216
7th " "	111	100	211
8th " "	102	108	210
9th " "	114	95	209
10th " "	110	98	208
11th " "	109	95	204
12th " "	111	85	196
13th " "	103	91	194
14th " "	104	88	192
15th " "	109	82	191
16th " "	99	84	183

TIME MATCHES.

Five competitions shot at Creedmoor in 1876. Distance, 200 yards. Third-class target. Any rifle (magazine guns used as single-loaders). As many shots as possible to be fired within 30 seconds, and competitors to have two chances: the aggregate score of both rounds to be counted.

1st Competition.—1st chance: the winner fired 8 shots and made 5 hits, scoring 18 points. 2d chance: the winner fired 8 shots and made 7 hits, scoring 19 points. Total, 37 points.

2d Competition.—1st chance: the winner fired 6 shots and made 4 hits, scoring 14 points. 2d chance: the winner fired 5 shots and made 5 hits, scoring 20 points. Total, 34 points.

3d Competition.—1st chance: the winner fired 9 shots and made 8 hits, scoring 25 points. 2d chance: the winner fired 9 shots and made 8 hits, scoring 27 points. Total, 52 points.

4th Competition.—1st chance: the winner fired 11 shots and made 9 hits, scoring 33 points. 2d chance: the winner fired 14 shots and made 13 hits, scoring 40 points. Total, 73 points.

5th Competition.—1st chance: the winner fired 14 shots and made 9 hits, scoring 24 points. 2d chance: the winner fired 14 shots and made 11 hits, scoring 39 points. Total, 63 points.

"TRAMP" MATCH.

Shot at Creedmoor during Fall Meeting of the N. R. A. of 1878. Teams of four men. Distance, 100 yards. Military rifles.

I.—As many shots as possible by file firing within *one minute*.

II.—Five volleys fired according to the tactics.

Target.—The figure of a Tramp (working as explained on page 50), having a 3-inch "Bull's-eye," 8-inch "Centre;" above the hips, "Inner;" remainder of figure, "Outer."

The winning team made an aggregate of 44 hits, scoring 135 points.

The second team made 47 hits, scoring 129 points.

SOLDIERS' MATCH.

Five competitions shot at Creedmoor in 1878. Teams of eight. Military rifles. Distance, 200 yards. Third-class targets (wood covered with paper).

I.—Firing by file. Time not to exceed two minutes from command, "Commence firing."

II.—Firing by volley. Five volleys for each team. Hits on target ascertained by counting the bullet-holes. A separate paper target for each team.

1st Match.—File firing: winning team made 31 hits, scoring 101 points. Volley firing: winning team made 30 hits, scoring 89 points. Total, 190 points.

2d Match.—File firing: winning team made 30 hits, scoring 88 points. Volley firing: winning team made 27 hits, scoring 89 points. Total, 177 points.

3d Match.—File firing: winning team made 37 hits, scoring 124 points. Volley firing: winning team made 30 hits, scoring 100 points. Total, 224 points.

4th Match.—File firing: winning team made 40 hits, scoring 136 points. Volley firing: winning team made 35 hits, scoring 102 points. Total, 238 points.

5th Match.—File firing: winning team made 38 hits, scoring 129 points. Volley firing: winning team made 33 hits, scoring 104 points. Total, 233 points.

AGGREGATE PRIZES.

Winners of prizes offered for highest aggregate score in the following matches of Fall Meetings of the N. R. A. at Creedmoor.

1875.

E. H. SANFORD.

		200 yds.	500 yds.	Total.
Match X. 500 yards. 7 shots. Military rifle				30
" VI. 200 and 500 yards. 5 shots each distance. Military rifle		21	20	41
" IV. 200 and 500 yards. 5 shots each distance. Military rifle		20	24	44
			Aggt.	115

FRANK HYDE.

		500 yds.	600 yds.	Total.
Match III. 200 yards. 7 shots. Creedmoor rifle				28
" XII. 500 and 600 yards. 7 shots each distance. Creedmoor rifle		32	30	62
" XIV. 800 and 1000 yards. 10 shots each distance. Creedmoor rifle (800 yds. / 1000 yds.)		43	42	85
			Aggt.	175

1876.

W. H. DEWAR.

		200 yds.	500 yds.	Total.
Match IV. 500 yards. 7 shots. Military rifle				32
" VII. 200 and 500 yards. 5 shots each distance. Military rifle		20	21	41
" IX. 200 and 500 yards. 5 shots each distance. Military rifle		17	21	38
			Aggt.	111

E. H. SANFORD.

		200 yds.	600 yds.	1000 yds.	Total.
Match II.	200 yards. 7 shots. Sporting rifle............				25
" V.	200, 600, and 1000 yards. 10 shots each distance. Creedmoor rifle................	42	47	44	133
" XII.	800 and 1000 yards. 10 shots each distance. Creedmoor rifle.......................	800 yds. 48	1000 yds. 49		97

Aggt. 255

1877.

JOHN HENWOOD.

		200 yds.	500 yds.	Total.
Match V.	500 yards. 7 shots. Military rifle.............			30
" VI.	200 and 500 yards. 5 shots each distance. Military rifle......	20	18	38
" IX.	200 and 500 yards. 5 shots each distance. Military rifle......	20	23	43

Aggt. 111

FRANK HYDE.

		200 yds.	600 yds.	1000 yds.	Total.
Match II.	200 yards. 7 shots. Sporting rifle.............				26
" III.	200, 600, and 1000 yards. 10 shots each distance........	41	48	37	126
" XIII.	1000 yards. 30 shots. Creedmoor rifle......				135

Aggt. 287

1878.

JOHN CORRY.

		200 yds.	500 yds.	Total.
Match IX. 500 yards. 7 shots. Military rifle.				30
" XI. 200 and 500 yards. 5 shots each distance. Military rifle.		17	22	39
" XIII. 200 and 500 yards. 5 shots each distance. Military rifle.		21	18	39
			Aggt.	108

FRANK HYDE.

	200 yds.	600 yds.	1000 yds.	Total.
Match II. 200 yards. 7 shots.				26
" V. 200, 600, and 1000 yards. 10 shots each distance.	37	49	45	131
" XXVI. 1000 yards. 30 shots.				143
			Aggt.	300

FOREIGN MATCHES.

COMPETITIONS FOR THE

ELCHO CHALLENGE SHIELD.

Since 1870. Shot annually at Wimbledon, England. Teams of eight, representing respectively England, Scotland, and Ireland. Distances, 800, 900, and 1000 yards. Fifteen shots at each distance. Any rifles.

(Old targets. Highest possible team aggregate, 1440 points.)

	800 yds.	900 yds.	1000 yds.	Aggt.
1870.—England, score	420	387	359	1166
Ireland, "	392	359	353	1104
Scotland, "	387	359	357	1103

		800 yds.	900 yds.	1000 yds.	Aggt.
1871.—England, score	....	403	420	381	1204
Ireland, "	....	400	410	370	1180
Scotland, "	....	379	410	361	1150
1872.—England, "	....	407	421	355	1183
Scotland, "	....	416	392	364	1172
Ireland, "	....	394	405	353	1152
1873.—Ireland, "	....	426	379	390	1195
England, "	....	418	377	380	1175
Scotland, "	....	405	371	352	1128

(New targets. Highest possible team aggregate, 1800 points.)

		800 yds.	900 yds.	1000 yds.	Aggt.
1874.—Scotland, score	....	504	488	445	1437
England, "	....	483	462	460	1405
Ireland, "	....	465	473	440	1378
1875.—Ireland, "	....	502	527	477	1506
Scotland, "	....	498	511	494	1503
England, "	....	515	504	483	1502
1876.—England, "	....	489	490	484	1463
Scotland, "	....	504	503	451	1458
Ireland, "	....	479	449	454	1382
1877.—Ireland, "	....	543	517	508	1568
England, "	....	513	478	473	1464
Scotland, "	....	530	470	439	1439
1878.—Ireland, "	..	540	535	535	1610
England, "	....	534	521	505	1560
Scotland, "	....	532	523	497	1552

THE QUEEN'S PRIZE.

Matches, since 1874, shot for annually at Wimbledon. FIRST STAGE, 200, 500, and 600 yards. Seven shots at each distance. Government rifle. Highest possible aggregate score, 105 points.—SECOND STAGE, 800, 900, and 1000 yards. Seven shots each distance. Government rifle.

							Aggt.
1874.—							
1st Stage.	Winner,	Corpl. Young,	score..............				87
2d "	"	Pvt. Atkinson,	"	28	23	13	64
1875.—							
1st "	"	Pvt. Innes,	"				90
2d "	"	Capt. Pearse,	"	30	28	15	73
1876.—							
1st "	"	Pvt. Burgess,	"				86
2d "	"	Sgt. Pullman,	"	23	28	23	74
1877.—							
1st "	"	Corpl. Betts,	"				92
2d "	"	Pvt. Jamieson,	"	22	23	25	70
1878.—							
1st "	"	Pvt. Lowe,	"				95
2d "	"	Pvt. Rae,	"	30	23	25	78

THE END.

SPORTS BY LAND AND SEA.

HOW TO GET STRONG, AND HOW TO STAY SO. By WILLIAM BLAIKIE. Illustrated. 16mo, Cloth.

THE RIFLE CLUB AND RANGE. By A. H. WESTON. Illustrated. 16mo, Cloth.

FISHING IN AMERICAN WATERS. By GENIO C. SCOTT. A New Edition, containing Parts Six and Seven, on Southern and Miscellaneous Fishes. Illustrated. 8vo, Cloth, $3 50.

PRAIRIE AND FOREST: A Description of the Game of North America, with Personal Adventures in their Pursuit. By PARKER GILLMORE. Illustrated. 12mo, Cloth, $1 50.

THE FISHING TOURIST: Angler's Guide and Reference Book. By CHARLES HALLOCK. Illustrated. Crown 8vo, Cloth, $2 00.

STARBOARD AND PORT: The "Nettie" Along Shore. A Summer's Yacht Cruise along the Coasts of Maine and Labrador. By GEORGE H. HEPWORTH. Illustrated. 12mo, Cloth, $1 75.

HUNTER'S LIFE IN AFRICA. Five Years of a Hunter's Life in the far Interior of South Africa. With Notices of the Native Tribes, and Anecdotes of the Chase of the Lion, Elephant, Hippopotamus, Giraffe, Rhinoceros, &c. By R. GORDON CUMMING. 2 vols., 12mo, Cloth, $3 00.

THE CANOE AND FLYING PROA; or, Cheap Cruising and Safe Sailing. By W. L. ALDEN. With Illustrations. 32mo, Paper, 25 cents; Cloth, 40 cents.

MANUAL OF PHYSICAL EXERCISES. By WILLIAM WOOD. Copiously Illustrated. 12mo, Cloth, $1 50.

I GO A-FISHING. By WILLIAM C. PRIME. Crown 8vo, Cloth, $2 50; Half Calf, $4 50.

THE PRAIRIE TRAVELLER. With Maps, Illustrations, and Itineraries of the Principal Routes between the Mississippi and the Pacific. By Brevet Brig.-General R. B. MARCY, U.S.A. Published by Authority of the War Department. 16mo, Cloth, $1 00.

FOREST LIFE AND FOREST TREES. Comprising Winter Camp-Life among the Loggers, and Wild-Wood Adventure. With Descriptions of Lumbering Operations on the various Rivers of Maine and New Brunswick. By J. S. SPRINGER. Illustrated. 12mo, Cloth, $1 50.

AFRICAN HUNTING. African Hunting from Natal to the Zambesi, including Lake Ngami, the Kalahari Desert, &c., from 1852 to 1860. By WILLIAM CHARLES BALDWIN, F.R.G.S. Illustrated. 12mo, Cloth, $1 50.

NIMROD OF THE SEA; or, The American Whaleman. By WILLIAM M. DAVIS. Illustrated. 12mo, Cloth, $2 00.

PUBLISHED BY HARPER & BROTHERS, N. Y.

☞ *Any of the above works sent by mail, postage prepaid, to any part of the United States, on receipt of price.*

WOOD'S PHYSICAL EXERCISES.

MANUAL OF PHYSICAL EXERCISES: comprising Gymnastics, Rowing, Skating, Fencing, Cricket, Calisthenics, Sailing, Swimming, Sparring, Base-Ball, together with Rules for Training and Sanitary Suggestions. By WILLIAM WOOD, Instructor in Physical Education, and Director of Exercises in the Young Men's Christian Association of New York. Third Edition, enlarged. Profusely Illustrated. 12mo, Cloth, $1 50.

His rules are carefully and judiciously given, and he shows great familiarity with the physiological and hygienic considerations involved in the topic of which he treats.—*Albany Evening Journal.*

Mr. Wood has executed his work with all the thoroughness and ability which the public had a right to look for from such an expert in physical exercises as himself.—*Brooklyn Times.*

A very comprehensive treatise, and it is to be heartily commended to the public.—*Presbyterian*, Phila.

A valuable repertory of concise information on all the subjects whereof it treats. Those in quest of health and strength may reap benefit from its perusal.—*Methodist*, N. Y.

A useful and commendable work. Mr. Wood is an experienced instructor in gymnastic and athletic exercises, and he is admirably qualified to write upon physical education.—*Boston Transcript.*

Written by a complete master of the various arts enumerated, in succinct and forcible manner, and containing many valuable suggestions about diet, dress, personal cleanliness, and exercise in relation to perfect health and physical development. * * * It may be perused with profit by the wisest and best.—*Christian Advocate*, N. Y.

PUBLISHED BY HARPER & BROTHERS, N. Y.

☞ HARPER & BROTHERS *will send the above work by mail, postage prepaid, to any part of the United States, on receipt of* $1 50.

www.ingramcontent.com/pod-product-compliance
Lightning Source LLC
Chambersburg PA
CBHW020250170426
43202CB00008B/303